DATE DUE			

389502

921
Mui

Goldstein, Natalie.

John Muir

10/20/16

JOHN MUIR

Conservation Heroes

Conservation Heroes

JOHN MUIR

Natalie Goldstein

CHELSEA HOUSE
An Infobase Learning Company

John Muir

Copyright ©2011 by Infobase Learning

Chelsea House
An imprint of Infobase Learning
132 West 31st Street
New York, NY 10001

Library of Congress Cataloging-in-Publication Data
Goldstein, Natalie.
 John Muir / Natalie Goldstein.
    p. cm. — (Conservation heroes)
 Includes bibliographical references and index.
 ISBN 978-1-60413-945-7 (hardcover)
 1. Muir, John, 1838–1914—Juvenile literature. 2. Naturalists—United
States—Biography—Juvenile literature. 3. Conservationists—United States—
Biography—Juvenile literature. I. Title.
 QH31.M9G65 2010
 333.72092—dc22
 [B]   2010030582

Text design by Annie O'Donnell
Cover design by Takeshi Takahashi
Composition by Newgen North America
Cover printed by Bang Printing, Brainerd, MN
Book printed and bound by Bang Printing, Brainerd, MN
Date printed: March 2011
Printed in the United States of America

10 9 8 7 6 5 4 3 2 1

This book is printed on acid-free paper.

Contents

Muir's Turning Point

John Muir's life had barely begun. He was 29, still a young man, yet here he was lying in bed in a darkened room. He had been in his dim and gloomy room for weeks, lying as still as possible for fear that he might lose his sight forever. Still, Muir's doctors were optimistic about his recovery as long as their patient lay still and quiet.

Muir had emigrated from Scotland to the United States with his family. He had escaped grueling labor on his family's Wisconsin farm by finding employment in a woodworking factory, where he had his accident.

Muir was vigorous and energetic, so being confined to bed was a real trial for him. However, Muir realized that his accident was also a gift—a gift of time for quiet contemplation. Lying alone in the dark, he could think seriously about what he really wanted to do with his life.

John Muir saw that his life up to that time had revealed his two greatest assets. The one he cherished most was his overwhelming love of the natural world. When he was out in nature, he was filled

Naturalist, explorer, and writer John Muir poses in this image taken circa 1875, when he was 37.

with an immense joy and experienced a spiritual connection to all things wild and untamed. His other strength lay in his creativity and mechanical skills, which made him a great inventor. He had invented all sorts of useful and amazing mechanical devices. In the America of his time—it was 1867—it was his inventive creativity

WORKING WITH WOOD

By the mid-nineteenth century, large machines were often used to make wooden objects. Many large machines were run by a huge flywheel that kept the machine turning while the wood was cut or shaped. Some of these woodworking flywheels were so big that the factories had to be built around them.

Factories that made small items used smaller machines powered by foot pedals or a small engine. Both small and large machines had belts that kept the machine parts turning. Huge belts connected the flywheel to saws or other moving parts on large machines. Belts also connected pedals or engines to saws, lathes, or other woodworking tools. Some items were finished with hand tools, such as planes or finishing files, after they had been shaped by the machines.

This scene in the woodworking shop at Tuskegee Institute, taken in 1906, shows some of the typical large machines used to craft work in Muir's time as a woodworker.

that other people valued. His current job in the largest woodworking factory in Indianapolis, Indiana, paid an excellent salary. However, it was working in this factory that had landed him in his current predicament.

The owners of the woodworking firm of Osgood & Smith had hired Muir to be just another working man who would daily turn out the required number of broom handles, carriage wheels, barrels, and other wooden items they manufactured. Yet it did not take long for the partners to recognize that Muir was no ordinary laborer, but a talented inventor and businessman. They promoted him to foreman and gave him a hefty raise in salary. Muir noticed how inefficient the factory was, and his employers encouraged him to redesign the factory's equipment to make it more efficient. Muir was asked to evaluate the factory's efficiency and to make recommendations on how it could be improved. His bosses respected and valued his business skills and treated him almost as an equal.

Muir had his fateful accident while working late one evening installing a new belt on one of the woodworking machines. Muir used a long, thin file to reach into the machine to loosen some heavy lacings that held the old belt. At first, the stubborn lacings refused to give, so Muir really put some muscle into freeing them with the file. After one particularly hard pull, the lacings suddenly sprang apart. Muir's hand flew upward, and the sharp point of the file he was holding plunged into his right eye. For an instant, Muir was too stunned to move. He cupped the eye with his hand and, after the initial shock had passed, walked to a nearby window to assess the damage. Slowly, Muir removed the hand from over his eye. As he gazed at his palm, drops of fluid from the inside of his eye dripped into it. Muir's shock turned to horror as he watched his punctured eye empty its sight-giving fluid into his palm. Within minutes, Muir's vision in that eye disappeared.

Somehow, Muir managed to stagger back to the rooms he shared with a fellow worker. Within an hour or so, the shock from his injury sent him trembling to bed. As he lay shaking and terrified, the vision in his left eye faded, too. John Muir was totally blind.

WHAT'S IN AN EYE?

The sharp file that entered John Muir's eye pierced the edge of the cornea, the transparent, protective covering over the eye. Luckily, it did not damage the eye's most vital parts. The pupil, which gets bigger and smaller to control the amount of light entering the eye, was unharmed. The eye lens, which helps focus the image, was

(continues)

Inside the Eye

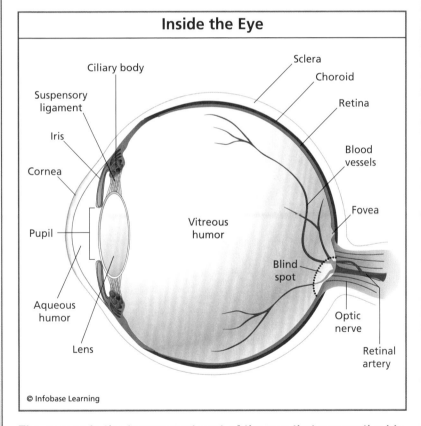

© Infobase Learning

The cornea is the transparent part of the eye that covers the iris, pupil, and lens. Along with the lens, the cornea is necessary to refract light.

(continued)

also not damaged. Thankfully, the retina and optic nerve were also untouched, so they were still able to send information about the visual image from the eye to the brain, which interprets the image. The aqueous humor (also called aqueous fluid) is fluid that fills the center of the eye, and it is vital in giving the eye its shape and allowing other parts of the eye to function properly. Fortunately, the fluid can be replaced by the body. That is why Muir's injured eye eventually healed and he regained most of his sight.

The next day, a doctor came to examine Muir's wounded eye. He assured his patient that there was every reason to believe that his right eye would heal well enough for its vision to return—though it would never be as acute as it had been before the accident. The left eye, the doctor said, had lost its sight as a form of "sympathetic reaction" to the shock the right eye had suffered. The doctor was confident that during the course of healing, the left eye would regain its sight and Muir would be able to see from it as well as ever. Muir breathed a sigh of relief. The beauty of the world might not be closed to him forever after all.

In the following weeks, which Muir spent in bed as his eyes healed, he thought long and hard about what had happened to him—and what he should do about it. Muir had to earn a living. He had come to Indianapolis to find work, and his extraordinary mechanical talent had been recognized and well rewarded. In the biography *John Muir: Rediscovering America,* author Frederick Turner notes that Muir had written to his family that "[N]ow that I am among machines I begin to *feel* that I have some talent that way, and so I almost think, unless things change soon, I shall turn my whole mind into that channel." Muir understood that he could very well end up rich and successful—in society's view—if he dedicated himself to business. Yet as he lay in his dark room, Muir knew that this was not what his heart was telling him to do.

As Muir took stock of his life, he realized he had reached a "fork in the road," and he had to decide for himself which path to follow. He was good at business and mechanical invention, but while doing this work, his soul ached to escape into the glorious wilderness. He was never happy with workaday tasks because some essential part of him yearned to be free and become one with wild nature. Muir found the everyday world of work and creature comforts to be shallow and unfulfilling. It was unspoiled nature that made his heart sing and his soul glad. Yet Muir questioned the practicality of this idea: What kind of profession is "nature lover" or "mountain man?" How would he earn a living? Even a wandering naturalist sometimes needed to buy food and clothing. Where would the money come from?

John Muir wrestled with this problem as the weeks passed, weighing one option against the other. As time passed, he realized that his mind kept turning back to his soul's desire. When he lost his sight he was not worried about no longer being able to work in a factory, but instead despaired that he might never again see the glories of nature. Muir was coming to understand that he had to live in accord with his soul's calling. Come what may—poverty, loneliness, the disapproval of others—he would live the way his heart told him to live.

Muir wrote to Jeanne Carr, his best friend, to tell her about his predicament. Of all the people he met in his life, Carr had the deepest understanding of Muir's soul. After the accident, she wrote to him: "I have often in my heart wondered what God was training you for. He gave you the 'eye within the eye,' to see in all natural objects the realized ideas of His mind. . . . He made you more an individualized existence than is common, and by your very nature, removed you from common temptations. He will surely place you where your work is."

When his sight returned sufficiently to allow him to venture out, Muir walked to a nearby meadow that was covered with new spring flowers. His heart rejoiced. He knew he had made the right decision. He would follow his soul's calling to go into the wilderness to become one with all of God's earthly creation.

When he was fully recovered, Muir gave notice that he would be leaving his job. His bosses offered him more money to stay, but Muir graciously turned them down. John Muir had other plans—a 1,000-mile (1,609-kilometer) walk he had been yearning to take for years.

Childhood in Dunbar

John Muir was born on April 21, 1838. He and his brother David were the eldest sons among the seven Muir children. The boys shared a small, narrow bedroom on the top floor of their small, narrow house in Dunbar, a Scottish port town on the North Sea. Most nights, after going to bed, the boys played at "voyaging" under the covers. They would imagine what it would be like to sail the world on one of the fine ships that docked at Dunbar. They whispered excitedly about the strange and dazzling places they would visit and of the fantastical adventures they would have. They would go to America or to the South Seas, see wondrous things and do amazing and heroic deeds. They whispered together for hours until their eyes drooped shut and they finally fell asleep.

The boys also liked to test their bravery by playing "scootchers," or pranks. It was usually Johnnie Muir, the older boy, who came up with up the most outlandish "scootchers." One dark and stormy night, for example, Johnnie challenged David to enter an unused bedroom the children believed was haunted by a ghost. Another night, Johnnie dared his brother to follow him out a window and

John Muir's birthplace, pictured in June 2010, is now a tourist site in Dunbar, Scotland. Muir's family lived in the three-story stone building at 126 High Street, in which his father also operated a successful food and grain store.

onto the roof. David was too scared, but John scrambled up to the rooftop where he swung his arms at the stars while his nightshirt billowed around him like a white sail.

Had either of the boys been caught at these pranks, they probably would have been whipped. Their fantasies and "scootchers" were the only relief they found at home from the grim harshness of their family life. Daniel Muir, their father, was a very strict, religious, and humorless man who believed that fun, games, and fantasy were sinful. Daniel tried to limit the boys' play to the small, dark, and narrow "garden" at the back of the house. As soon as the boys were old enough, however, they escaped through the garden door to find adventure and fun in the wider world of Dunbar.

DAILY LIFE
At Home

Life in the Muir home was ruled by the father's strict religious ideas. The family awoke so early, they ate their breakfast of oatmeal and milk in the dark. After a morning at school, the children returned home for a lunch of boiled mutton (sheep), vegetable broth, and a barley scone (bread). At the end of the school day, they had a tea-less tea, or half a scone with a cup of warm water mixed with milk and sugar. Dinner usually consisted of a boiled potato and yet another scone.

Daniel Muir insisted that meals be taken in absolute silence so the family could concentrate on thanking the Lord for their food. After dinner, he led the family in lengthy prayers in which he begged God that none in his family should fall into temptation. Then everyone went to bed.

On most days, Daniel tested his children on their Bible learning. Each child had to memorize and then be able to recite a passage from the Bible. Each child had to learn a set number of Bible verses every day and recite them accurately from memory for their father the following night. Any child who made a mistake or forgot a verse was whipped. *Nature Writings,* a collection of Muir's own writings, quotes Muir's autobiography in which he wrote that by age eleven he had memorized all of the New Testament and most of the Old Testament "by heart and by sore flesh."

At School

Johnnie Muir first entered school when he was three years old, a common practice in Scotland at the time. The Davel Brae School, a dark and forbidding place surrounded by a high wall, focused as

CALVINISM

Calvinism is a form of Protestant Christianity founded by John Calvin in the sixteenth century. Calvin taught that people should live according to the literal word of the Bible. Calvinism teaches that since the Fall, when Adam and Eve were expelled from the Garden of Eden, all humans are sinful and corrupt. Although their actions, too, are sinful, it is every person's duty to work hard as a way of serving God on Earth. Yet no matter how hard one works, one's inborn sin cannot be erased. God may choose to give his grace to selected individuals, but nothing one does can influence God's choice. Calvinism's negative view of human nature makes it a harsh and rigid religion that forbids the more lighthearted human pursuits.

French pastor John Calvin was an early leader in the branch of Christian theology that became known as Calvinism.

much on hard discipline as it did on reading and writing. Johnnie's teacher, Mungo Siddons, got his young pupils to learn mainly through threats and whippings.

Johnnie Muir did well enough in his lessons to graduate to the local grammar school when he was about eight years old. Here, regular whippings were used to beat Latin, French, English, arithmetic, spelling, and geography into the boys' heads. Muir described the school's approach in his 1913 autobiography: "We were simply driven point blank against our books like soldiers against the enemy . . . If we failed in any part, however slight, we were whipped." The grammar school, like Muir's father, operated on the Calvinist idea that people were sinful and only hard work, enforced with physical punishment, could steer them along the right path.

At Play

After school or on Saturdays, if the weather was fine, Johnnie and his friends enjoyed themselves by walking along the shore and collecting shells or sailing their small wooden boats. Every boy whittled his own tiny ship, which the friends raced in the shallow water near the shore. Sometimes they prowled the harbor, admiring the magnificent sailing ships docked there. If they were lucky, they would occasionally meet sailors who told them yarns about the sea, about far-off places and wonderful adventures, as well as tales of terrible storms and shipwrecks and of miraculous rescues.

One of the boys' favorite pastimes was climbing up to Dunbar Castle, an ancient building that is nearly 1,000 years old and now mostly rubble. There, they acted out the famous battles that had been fought there. These war games were great fun, especially as the boys made sure that the Scots always beat the English (even though history had turned out differently). Their play was made even more exciting by the castle's reputation for being haunted.

The summer vacation from school was Johnnie's favorite time because it was then that he could wander far and wide beyond Dunbar and into the countryside. Johnnie loved nothing more than to roam the broad, green open spaces of the Lammermuirs outside of Dunbar. It was during these explorations that Muir first realized

DUNBAR CASTLE

Dunbar Castle, built in the twelfth century, stands on a headland extending into the North Sea. It was built by a powerful Scottish clan as a fortress to keep out invaders. In 1338, the English attacked the castle but were repelled. Later, the Scots destroyed the castle to prevent the English from taking control of it. In 1494, the castle was rebuilt by the Scots, but it—and the town of Dunbar—was soon after burned down by invading English troops.

In 1566, Mary, Queen of Scots took refuge in the castle after some Scottish lords murdered her top advisor. One year later, she again used the castle to protect herself from rebellious Scots who had killed her unpopular and foolish husband, Darnley. Mary's third husband, Bothwell, also took refuge in the castle, but he was forced to surrender it to James Stuart, Earl of Moray, who ordered the castle to be dismantled. Dunbar Castle was almost completely destroyed in the early nineteenth century, when its stone was used to build a new harbor. Little remains of this ancient fortress.

The ruins of Dunbar Castle sit in Dunbar Harbor. Only one tower of the castle, built with red stone, remains standing.

how much he loved nature. He never tired of tramping alone for hours over the Lammermuirs seeking out new vistas, new plants and animals, and new insights into the natural world. The "wanderlust," or love of wandering, that Muir developed as a child would grow in him throughout his life.

SUDDENLY, A NEW LIFE

In the winter of 1849, out of a clear blue sky, Daniel Muir announced to his family that they were moving to America. It is likely that even his wife, Anne, knew nothing about this move, which her husband had been planning in secret. She was understandably upset, and her parents, in turn, insisted that she and the younger children stay behind in Dunbar until Daniel and the two oldest boys were settled and had built a house for the family in the New World.

Why did Daniel Muir decide to uproot his family so suddenly and move to such a far-away place? It was not because he had heard word of riches found during the California Gold Rush, which was underway at that time. Like many immigrants before him, Daniel Muir moved to America because of its religious freedom. He had converted to a Protestant sect, or group, called the Disciples of Christ. This strict sect, he believed, taught the true meaning of Christianity, and its members lived a "pure" and disciplined life that brought them closer to God. As there were few Disciples of Christ in Dunbar, Daniel decided to move to one of the Disciples of Christ communities that were sprouting up in America. Daniel had contacted important members of his new church who told him that many Disciples of Christ had settled in Wisconsin. Though he had only the vaguest understanding of American geography, Daniel decided to settle his family in Wisconsin.

The Voyage

On February 19, 1849, Johnnie and David left Dunbar and traveled to Glasgow, Scotland, where they boarded a ship for New York. Unlike his mother and grandparents, Johnnie was overjoyed at the prospect of a new life in America. He had heard countless tales of

The low, rolling hills that make up the Lammermuirs provide a great deal of open space in a beautiful, natural setting.

the wonders of America's endless wilderness. He could barely contain his excitement at the thought of the adventures he would have in the wilds of Wisconsin.

Though the crossing was a hardship for many, Johnnie was too happy to notice. The eleven-year-old-boy gazed at the Atlantic waves, imagining the delights of his new life. He later wrote that the crossing was "a glorious six-week holiday" with no school, no strict rules, and—best of all—no whippings.

On April 5, 1849, the Muirs' ship docked in New York City. Daniel took no notice of the great city, but immediately booked passage on a boat going up the Hudson River to Albany. There, the Muirs boarded another boat on the Erie Canal that took them to Buffalo in western New York. In Buffalo, the gateway to the Midwest, Daniel and his sons boarded a steamer that, five days later, brought them to Milwaukee, Wisconsin. The last leg of the trip turned out to be the most difficult because it required them to take a long, hard journey overland across the prairie. Daniel paid a farmer to haul him and his sons—sitting atop bushels of wheat—to the town of Kingston, a village located about 100 miles (161 km) northwest of Milwaukee. The travelers were shaken and bruised as the ox-cart trundled over the rough grassland.

A New Home

When they arrived at the tiny hamlet of Kingston, Daniel Muir met a fellow Scotsman and Disciple of Christ who helped him look for suitable farmland. Daniel Muir bought 80 acres (32.3 hectares) of open woodland 6 miles (9.6 km) from Kingston. The land had woods, a meadow, and a brook that flowed into a small lake. The Muirs decided to call their farm Fountain Lake.

Daniel had his boys clear and plow some land and plant a few crops to keep them all fed through the coming winter. The boys also helped build a small shack to live in. Come the spring, they all began work on a larger, more permanent house. In 1850, Anne Muir and the younger children arrived and moved into the eight-room log house. It was plain, but it was sturdy. John Muir's American life had begun.

How Farming
Builds Character

Johnnie Muir's dreams of adventure in the wilds of America were crushed by his life on the family farm. These youthful years were among the grimmest of his life. The work was unrelenting and nearly killed him. His relationship with his father grew combative and bitter. Yet these Wisconsin farm years also shaped Johnnie's character and gave him the immense strength—both physical and mental—that would serve him well in his future life.

FOUNTAIN LAKE

Like most farmers in the area, Daniel Muir planted wheat as his cash crop. Of course, before a farmer can plant anything, the land must be cleared of trees and other vegetation. For months on end, it was Johnnie who wielded the axe or saw that cleared the land of trees. It was mainly 12-year-old Johnnie who sweated and strained to dig the enormous, deep tree roots out of the soil.

As the oldest son, it fell to Johnnie to break up the soil using a wooden plow whose handles were almost taller than he was. By

This illustration depicts the Muirs's first Wisconsin home at Fountain Lake.

the end of the day, the overworked boy was hobbling like an old man. After supper, it was Johnnie's task to bring the cows back to the barn and feed the horses. He would then say prayers and go to bed. The next day—and the ones after that—were the same. Every spring, these backbreaking chores fell to Johnnie Muir.

Summers were even worse. The southern Wisconsin farm was frequently baked by the murderous heat and humidity of the corn-belt plains. Johnnie was up before dawn, feeding and watering the farm animals. The rest of the day he spent cultivating and weeding the vast sun-blasted fields of wheat in temperatures that often topped 100°F (37.8°C). There was one shade tree at the edge of the field, but Daniel Muir forbade his children from cooling off in its shade. No breaks were allowed during work time. The children were not even allowed to speak to each other while they labored. The only relief might come if evening chores were finished early. As the sun sank in the sky, Johnnie and David might be able to snatch an hour for themselves and row out onto the lake to fish or just relax.

Harvesting the wheat was the hardest work of all. Wheat has to be harvested at just the right time, or it will go bad. At harvest time, the family woke at 4:00 A.M. and hurried out to the fields, where they hand-cut and bound the shafts of wheat with hardly a break for meals. They kept at it until sundown, working furiously 17 hours a day to get the job done in time. Harvesting was done during the dog days of August, in sweltering weather. In his autobiography Muir wrote that the boys' "cotton shirts clung to our backs as wet with sweat as the bathing suits of swimmers."

Work eased a bit in autumn. There was still "stump-grubbing," which refers to the digging out of stubborn bits of tree stumps. John-nie also split wood and built fences. In winter, he made or repaired farming tools, tended the animals, split firewood, and did other tasks. If not for the biting cold, winter would have been a relatively easy season for Johnnie and the other Muir children.

Despite his relentless work routine, Johnnie stole what time he could to lose himself in the natural world outside the farm. Muir learned the names and habits of the local birds. He especially loved the crazed call of the loon. His heart opened to the arrival of the bluebirds in spring, followed by song sparrows and thrushes, and the bobolinks he especially adored. No matter what time of year it was, Johnnie managed to find time to go off on his own to explore and observe the animals and plants around his new home. On Sunday afternoons, after church or when his father was away preaching, Johnnie would wander the woods or meadows to soak up the beauties of nature. Sometimes, he joined other farm children to collect wild strawberries or huckleberries. His favorite place was the lake, where he could spend the whole afternoon lazing on the shore watching the water birds and bugs and the fish flicking through the shallows. Sometimes, if his father was not around,

Johnnie waded into the lake and splashed around in the cool, soothing water.

After eight years of brutal labor, the farm seemed to be doing fairly well. All the tree stumps had been dug up. All the fences had been built. So, most of the toughest tasks were done. Then, unbelievably, in 1857, Daniel Muir dropped another bombshell on his family: They were moving to another farm. The new farm was located about 5 miles (8 km) away, and Daniel thought its land was more fertile and would produce more wheat. The truth was that Daniel Muir, like most of his neighbors, did not understand how to farm in a way that kept the soil healthy. Instead of using techniques that improved the soil, the farming methods used in those days depleted it. As a result, the wheat crop declined over time. Like most Americans of his time, Daniel Muir acted as if new and fertile land were infinitely available. When one plot of land was worked out, a farmer just cleared new land, as if there was no end to the land itself.

HICKORY HILL FARM

John Muir was in despair. The dreadful, backbreaking work of clearing land again fell to him. He had thought he was through with this killing labor but, as he wrote in his autobiography, he realized he had to "begin all over again to clear and fence and break up other fields . . . doubling all the stunting, heartbreaking chopping, grubbing, stump-digging, rail-splitting, fence-building, barn-building, [and] house building" on the new farm. His father ordered to him to begin clearing the new field before the family moved. He obeyed.

Months of land clearing was followed by the construction of a sturdy, two-story farmhouse and a big barn. Once relocated at the farm they named Hickory Hill, Daniel Muir decided that he was old enough to retire from manual labor. From then on, all the hard work of farming was done by his children. How they resented him as he sat by a farmhouse window, watching to make sure they were

SAVING THE SOIL

Good farmers understand how to maintain healthy soil. They use different techniques for improving soil. One method is crop rotation, which involves planting different crops on different sections of the farm field each year. Planting the same crop on the same soil every year drains the soil of nutrients. So, one year, farmers will plant a section of field with wheat, and the next year they may plant that section of field with potatoes or another crop. Another technique was planting a "green manure," such as alfalfa, that was plowed into the soil to enrich it. Planting legumes, such as soybeans, also adds nutrients to the soil. Legumes have nodes on their roots that add needed nitrogen to the soil and thus make the soil more fertile. Finally, leaving one section of a field fallow, or unplanted, for one year, allows the soil to regenerate its nutrients.

Nitrogen-fixing bacteria (*Rhizobium*) nodules rest on the roots of a soybean plant.

Daniel Muir moved his family into this Wisconsin home at Hickory Hill in 1857.

working and not slacking. He still gave the orders, and his children were obliged to follow them.

Unfortunately, unlike the old farm, Hickory Hill had no lake or any other surface water. Therefore, Daniel ordered his eldest son to dig a well behind the farmhouse. Using only a pick and shovel, John dug deeper into the ground day by day. Only a short way down, he ran into a thick, hard layer of sandstone. Daniel Muir tried using explosives to blast through the rock, but he lacked the know-how, and the rock was barely scratched. Thus, Daniel ordered John to chip away at the layer of rock using the pick and other hand tools. Early each morning, John stepped into a bucket and was lowered into the narrow, nearly airless shaft. He chipped away at the rock, inch by inch, until lunchtime, when he was lifted out. After lunch, he was lowered back down into the hole again and left to smash away at the rock until sundown. One morning, when the hole had reached a depth of 80 feet (24 m), John was overcome by deadly carbon dioxide gas that had seeped into the shaft from the surrounding soil, and he immediately began to lose consciousness. His father shouted down to him to climb into the bucket. Somehow, John managed to do so, and when Daniel pulled him up out of the shaft, John was unconscious and could barely breathe. Even though John had almost died, his father gave him only a day and a half of bed rest to recover his strength. Then it was back to digging. Finally, at 90 feet (27 m), John struck water. John Muir never forgave his father, who had never offered to help out and who had never spent any time in that well.

A SELF-STYLED CHRISTIAN

John Muir was now a 20-year-old man who had been toughened by his years of hard labor. He was no longer whipped, but, for the most part, he continued to obey his father's orders. Still, Muir bristled at his father's tyranny, and this led to deep divisions between them. Muir resented his father's brutal and uncompromising authority. He also began to question the nature of his father's religion.

One blisteringly hot summer day, Daniel Muir rode one of the farm horses more than 24 miles (38 km) over sun-baked dirt roads to attend a revival meeting. When he got back, it was clear that the horse was dying from exhaustion. Muir would always remember how the horse suffered, how it trailed after the children, bleeding from the nostrils and gasping for breath, silently begging for some form of relief as it was dying. A while later, Daniel Muir emerged from the farmhouse and shot the animal.

In his later writings, Muir used this incident as an example of how a self-professed Christian could act in a decidedly un-Christian way. Muir asserted that cruelty, or even indifference, to other living creatures—to any part of God's creation—was a betrayal of Christ's true teachings. Muir condemned the attitude of most Christians who saw the land they farmed, the trees they felled, and the animals they used, hunted, or slaughtered as mere commodities, or economic goods, to be used for human benefit. John Muir's soul was one with nature and the creation, and he saw God in all things. In Muir's view, if everything is God then every life has innate value and all life deserves to be honored. This, Muir felt, was true Christianity. He would always identify himself as a Christian, for he loved Christ and his teachings, but he broke completely from the attitudes of most mainstream church-goers.

SELF-EDUCATION

Daniel Muir distrusted any book other than the Bible. Yet when John asked his father for permission to buy a book on mathematics, the elder Muir agreed. He thought that the study of math would help John learn about the business of farming.

John devoured the math book and easily understood its concepts. That one book made him realize how starved he had been intellectually. He spent almost all his time in a family where books were not allowed. He rarely saw his few friends, but those he saw did not read books either.

However, Muir was able to satisfy his hunger for learning when he discovered that two neighboring families had brought books with them from Scotland. They were glad to lend their books to John Muir. Muir read books about history. He also loved great literature, particularly novels and poetry. He was particularly influenced by the Romantic poets who, like him, saw God's spirit in nature and were inspired by it. Muir was also strongly moved by memoirs written by explorers who had traveled to the world's wildest places. He dared to hope that one day he might follow in their footsteps.

Muir also took a deep interest in books about nature, especially botany. He began collecting wild plants and bringing them home to study them along with his botany texts. Pretty soon, botany became an obsession. From this time forward, and for most of his life, Muir rarely walked the wilds without a plant press in his backpack. Over time, he collected and studied hundreds, maybe thousands, of plant species.

MUIR THE INVENTOR

Daniel Muir barely tolerated his son's studies, but he would not tolerate slacking off work at all. The younger Muir had to find some

HOW TO MAKE A PLANT PRESS

To make a plant press, you will need the following materials:

- 2 thin wooden boards, 8 x 10 inches (20 x 25 centimeters)
- corrugated cardboard (from packing boxes)
- a utility knife; watercolor paper or paper towels, 8 x 10 inches (20 x 25 cm)
- adjustable straps (webbing straps)

Once you have assembled the materials, take the following steps:

1. Have an adult use the utility knife to cut the cardboard into 8 x 10-inch (20 x 25 cm) sheets.
2. Assemble the plant press by first laying one board flat on a table. Then put a sheet of cardboard on top of it, followed by two sheets of watercolor paper or two paper towels on top of the cardboard. Keep adding sheets of cardboard and paper, ending with a sheet of cardboard and the second board at the top of the pile.
3. Place the straps around the layers of board and paper, one near the top, the other near the bottom. Make sure the straps are long enough so that they can be tightened across the top board.
4. Carefully lay the plant between the two sheets of watercolor paper or paper towels. Spread the plant out so that its parts lay flat. Carefully place the cardboard over the top sheet of watercolor paper or paper towel. Put the plant press together and tighten the straps.

time alone to read and study. He decided that early morning would be his private time. After going to bed exhausted one night, Muir woke up at 1:00 A.M. It immediately occurred to him that this was

Follow these steps for each individual plant. Keep the plants in the press for about a week, until they are dry. When you undo the plant press, the plants will be in perfect condition for you to look at, study, or mount as art.

A flower press is a useful tool that preserves plants for study or decoration. John Muir carried one with him to save plants he found for later examination.

his time—he had three hours to himself before farm work began. He rushed downstairs to the farmhouse cellar. He had an idea for making an alarm clock that would wake him up at 1:00 A.M. each day. Shaking from the cold, Muir cleared a work space among the sacks of stored potatoes. Using bits of wood and any other material

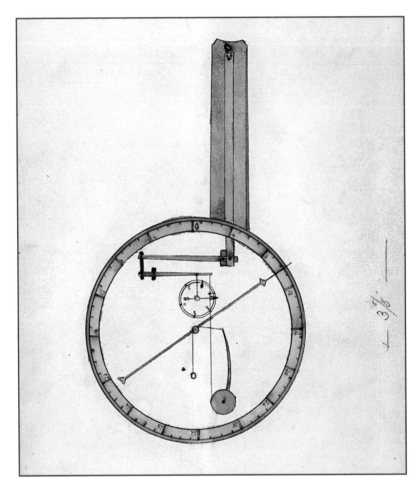

John Muir made a sketch of this thermometer before constructing it. He noted that the iron rod was about 3 feet (1 m) long and five-eighths of an inch (1.6 cm) in diameter. The scale was large enough to be read while he plowed the field near his house. Muir noted that it was sensitive enough to pick up the body heat of people standing 4 or 5 feet (1.2 or 1.5 cm) away from it.

he could find, John Muir invented his first alarm clock. It took weeks of effort and the first clock did not work very well, but Muir used it as a model for the large clocks he later built. Soon, Muir was designing and making several types of alarm clocks, and all of them worked.

Muir's most ingenious invention was his "alarm clock bed." This was a bed that had an alarm clock attached to it. When the clock hit the set time, another device would tip up the entire bed and throw the lazybones sleeper out onto the floor. Muir used this bed to make sure he got up on time in the middle of the night to continue working on his inventions.

It was clear to Muir that he had a talent for inventing things. After the alarm clocks and the tip-up bed, he invented new kinds of waterwheels, door locks, latches, water meters, barometers, and an automatic horse feeder. At first, Muir worried that his father would consider his inventions to be "sinful" and destroy them. However, Daniel Muir tolerated his son's creations so long as they did not interfere with work on the farm.

What Daniel Muir did not know was that his son's inventions would be his means of escaping the farm. By then, John Muir had despaired that he would ever be able to leave. Farming was the only work he knew. He had no other training and no formal education beyond Dunbar. He had no contact with the wider world, no place to go, and almost no money. His prospects for getting away from the farm to live his own life were not good. When he began inventing his machines, he had no idea that his creativity would eventually free him from the hard life of the farm.

On His Own at Last

In August 1860, one of John Muir's neighbors encouraged him to display his inventions at the upcoming Wisconsin State Fair in Madison. Muir wanted to go. He had a feeling that this might be his chance to start living his own life. As expected, John's father refused to help his son expand his horizons into the "evil and sinful" world beyond the farm. If John left, he could expect no help from his family. Muir was bitter that this would be his reward after 10 years of hard labor on the farm. Yet he was determined to go. He had saved about $15 from doing odd jobs on nearby farms and used that money to get to the fair. Muir packed some of his inventions into a cart and headed out into the world.

FRIENDS AND OPPORTUNITIES

It's hard to imagine the effect that the bustling city of Madison, Wisconsin, had on John Muir. This formerly isolated farm boy was a bit overwhelmed by all the buildings and the crowds of people who had come to the Wisconsin State Fair. At first, Muir was sure his work wouldn't be noticed. Yet, among all the prize bulls and machines on display, he was singled out for his ingenious inventions. A reporter from the *Journal,* a Madison newspaper, noted, "[I] saw some very ingenious specimens of mechanism, in the form of clocks made by Mr. John Muir. . . . The wheels moved with beautiful evenness. One [clock] registered not only hours, but minutes, seconds, and days of the month. The other [clock] was in the shape of a scythe . . . hung in a dwarf burr oak very tastefully ornamented. . . . We will venture to predict that few articles will attract as much attention as these products of Mr. Muir's ingenuity." John Muir and his inventions were a hit!

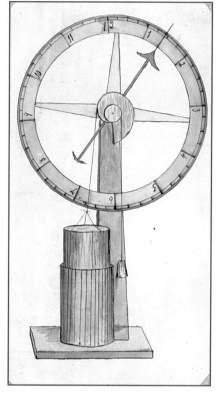

This watercolor illustration, made by John Muir circa 1863, shows one of his clocks.

By far, the most popular of Muir's inventions was the alarm-clock bed. Scores of children lined up to get a chance to be tipped out of the bed. For them it was like the most exciting ride at an amusement park. Among the bed-testers were the children of Jeanne Carr. She was impressed with how Muir patiently explained his invention to the children before giving each one of them a turn to try it out. Carr was the wife of a respected doctor and professor, and she had good connections with important people. She recommended that the fair's judges award a special cash prize to John Muir for his exhibit.

What most impressed Muir, however, was not the fair or its exhibits. It was the three large buildings located on the hill above the fair—they were the newly built facilities for the University of Wisconsin. Whenever he had the chance, Muir strolled among these impressive buildings and tried to figure out how he could become a student at the college. It saddened Muir to admit that this was unlikely to happen. He had no formal education beyond school in Dunbar and no money. How could he enroll in college? He set aside this ambition for the time being.

Muir rented a room in Madison and scratched out a meager living doing odd jobs as a handyman. He was so poor and had so little to eat, he became weak and sickly. He had to do something. So one day, Muir went to the university to talk with the school's acting director, John Sterling. Sterling remembered Muir's wonderful inventions and encouraged him to enroll at the school. Muir was surprised and relieved to hear how inexpensive the university fees were: Tuition for a 20-week term was only six dollars. Plus, room and board at the school cost only one dollar a week. If he could get a part-time job as a handyman, Muir could afford to enroll in college. He signed up for the new term.

COLLEGE MAN

At first, Muir had to attend college preparatory classes to improve his academic skills. At that time, most colleges had remedial courses to allow rural students with little formal education to get up to speed for college studies. When he completed this course, in February 1861, Muir began life as a college student. At first, he was drawn to courses in chemistry and geology. One of his professors in these subjects was Ezra Carr, Jeanne Carr's husband. Muir never decided on one particular course of study and took whatever courses appealed to him.

During summer break, Muir returned to the family farm and made a deal with his father: He would work on the farm, but only if he was paid. Daniel Muir grudgingly agreed to pay his son 75 cents a day for his labor. Muir saved every penny to cover his college expenses.

Back at school, Muir immersed himself in his studies. His fellow students loved to watch him hard at work at a "mechanical desk" he had invented. This odd object automatically moved his textbooks from their storage slot below to the desktop where Muir could study them.

Muir had never lost his love of plants and continued to tramp through woods and meadows carrying his plant press. At the beginning of the 1862 term, Muir met Milton Griswold, a fellow student who was studying botany. While they were out walking one day, Griswold gave Muir his first botany lesson, pointing out the similarity between the leaves of the pea plant and the locust tree. This likeness captivated Muir. He took samples of both plants back to his room and examined them closely. His excitement grew as he

THE STATE COLLEGE SYSTEM

In 1862, President Abraham Lincoln signed the Morrill Act, proposed by Vermont congressman Justin Smith Morrill, which provided federal funding for the establishment of land-grant, or state-run, colleges in each state. Land-grant colleges specialized in teaching agriculture and engineering, and also trained men for the military. The funds paid for the land and the construction of college buildings and dormitories, as well as for other necessary educational materials. Under its provision to "promote the liberal and practical education of the industrial classes in the several pursuits and professions in life," land-grant colleges could expand their curricula to include languages, literature, and the sciences.

The act was expanded several times. In 1914, a bill was added that funded agricultural cooperative extensions to conduct research into best agricultural practices and to engage in educational outreach programs for farmers and other interested citizens. Today, nearly every county has a cooperative extension run by the state's land-grant college.

realized that the study of botany combined his love of nature with the scientific study of its mysteries. For Muir, there was no conflict between spiritual nature and the science behind its forms. The

John Muir carved this wooden combination alarm clock and study desk around 1862, when he was a student at the University of Wisconsin-Madison. It is now on view at the Wisconsin Historical Society in Madison.

scientific understanding of nature simply revealed nature's grandeur more clearly. Muir was ecstatic. He felt he had found his life's work.

Muir took every course in botany that was offered at the university. He also enthusiastically studied geology. Many of Muir's courses were with Professor Carr, who liked Muir so much he invited him to his home to use his extensive library (and also to feed him large and wholesome home-cooked meals). During these visits to the professor's house, Muir formed his lifelong friendship with Jeanne Carr. Like Muir, she loved nature. For years, she acted as Muir's guiding light and sage advisor. Whenever he felt discouraged or confused, it was Jeanne Carr who lifted him with her devotion and encouragement.

BLOODY CIVIL WAR

Muir did his best to concentrate on his studies. Yet he could not ignore the rumors of war that swirled around him at the university. The southern states had begun to secede from the Union right after the election of Abraham Lincoln in 1860. Then, on April 12, 1861, Confederate troops in South Carolina fired on Fort Sumter, and the Civil War began. At first, there was no shortage of brave and patriotic university students and Wisconsin farm boys eager to sign up with the Union army. For many rural boys, the army was their escape from the miseries of farm labor. Thousands volunteered. Many students also dropped out of school to fight for the Union.

As the war wore on, however, the news from the front got worse. The Union suffered a terrible defeat at the battle of Bull Run (Manassas) and in other battles. Those who had signed up for a three-month stint in the army began to realize that they'd be fighting far longer than that. When people learned of the bloodbath at Antietam, which the Union claimed as a small "victory," they were sickened and horrified. The quick pulse of patriotism that had swelled the ranks of the Union army faded fast. President Lincoln was forced to institute a draft for all males between the ages of 20 and 45. Violent draft riots occurred throughout the North, even in normally sleepy rural Wisconsin. In July 1863, the first names drawn in the draft were announced, John Muir's was not among them, but he knew that he had to decide what to do—quickly.

Muir loved his new country, but he could not imagine killing for it. He revered human life, as he did all life, and knew it to be too valuable to be violently snuffed out no matter how just the cause. Muir refused to become a destroyer of life. He had to think of some way to avoid being drafted. He hated the thought of becoming a draft dodger, but finally he could see no other way out.

RICH MAN'S WAR, POOR MAN'S FIGHT

A rich man or his son did not have to worry if his name was drawn for the military draft. At that time, the law allowed anyone to "buy" his way out of the military by paying the government a $300 commutation fee that would release him from military service. A wealthy man could also choose to pay another man $300 to take his place in the Union army. Newspapers of the time were stuffed with ads placed by rich men seeking substitutes. Many desperately poor young men took the $300 and went to war, while the rich men who paid them stayed safely at home and went about their business. For the very poor, it was a risk they had to take. That is why the common people referred to the conflict as "the rich man's war, but the poor man's fight." It was mainly the poor who put their bodies on the line and suffered the consequences.

The Civil War remains the bloodiest conflict in U.S. history. Of the approximately 2.5 million Union soldiers who fought in the war, more than 360,000 died of wounds or disease. With Confederate casualties included, the total runs to about 620,000 men who perished.

After much soul-searching, John Muir decided to "skedaddle," the slang term for leaving the country to avoid the draft. He headed north to the Canadian wilderness.

CANADA

Muir left Madison and journeyed through northern Wisconsin into Canada. He felt free and spent months in solitary exploration of the forests and swamps around Lake Huron and Lake Ontario. When

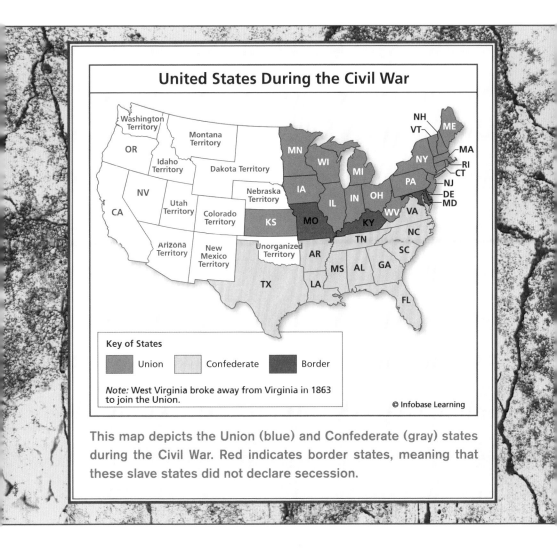

This map depicts the Union (blue) and Confederate (gray) states during the Civil War. Red indicates border states, meaning that these slave states did not declare secession.

necessity forced him to seek the company of his fellows, he was graciously welcomed into the homes of Canadians, who offered him food and a bed. For the most part, though, Muir was on his own. He spent long, lonesome weeks hiking through woodlands or wading through wetlands. Everywhere Muir went, he collected plants and preserved them in his plant press.

The weeks he spent slogging through swamps were especially isolating. The dark, dank bogs and wetlands were profoundly silent, which made Muir feel almost dead to the world. It was during these weeks that Muir reported that he realized that the "saturated wilderness . . . took no cognizance of the frenzied doings of humans." Nature, Muir realized, was totally indifferent to humans and their pursuits, or even to their survival. Though this realization was at first a bit unnerving, nature complete in itself soon brought him a sense of peace. Muir's own insignificance in the face of overwhelming nature helped him see himself as a small but unique and vital part of nature, and enabled him to achieve a true oneness with it.

Muir spent part of June 1864 with a farming family by the name of Campbell, where he earned a few dollars as a part-time farmhand. Still, he spent most of his time botanizing, examining, collecting, and studying plants. In July, he traveled to Niagara Falls, where he met up with his brother Dan. Dan knew a sawmill owner named William Trout in the tiny Canadian town of Meaford. Trout needed workers. Muir needed money and so, that fall, the brothers went to work at Trout's sawmill. The Muirs spent the winter working there, making rakes and brooms.

By 1865, Dan was homesick. The war had ended, so the draft was no longer a threat. Dan headed back to Wisconsin while Muir stayed on. He took the summer off to botanize and roam the woods, and then worked at the mill during the fall and winter. When, in February 1866, the factory burned to the ground during a blizzard, Muir saw that as a sign that his work there was done. Unfortunately though, Trout lost everything in the fire and could not pay Muir the $300 he owed him. Despite all the work he'd done, Muir was poor once again.

HEADING SOUTH

Muir returned to the United States and moved to Indianapolis, Indiana, where he got the job at Osgood & Smith's wood-working factory. What happened there—the accident that temporarily cost Muir his sight—set him on his life's path. The return of Muir's sight gave him even greater appreciation of nature. "The smallest plot of ground," Muir later wrote, "is in reality 10 thousand-fold too great for our comprehension, and we are at length lost, bewildered, overwhelmed in the immortal, shoreless, fathomless ocean of God's beauty."

Muir had earned good money at the factory, but it was time to live the life he was born for. He returned to his father's farm for the summer. That August, John Muir said good-bye to his family and the Wisconsin farm, which he would never see again. His parting from his mother and siblings was emotional. When Muir said good-bye to his father, Daniel Muir gruffly demanded that his oldest son pay him one gold piece to cover the cost of his food and lodging at the farm. Muir handed over the money.

John Muir also wrote a letter to Jeanne Carr: "I mean to start for the South tomorrow. . . . [I seem] doomed to be 'carried of the spirit into the wilderness,' I suppose. I wish I could be more moderate in my desires, but I cannot, and so there is no rest." Muir set out for Florida.

Seeking His Destiny

John Muir set off on his 1,000-mile (1,609-km) walk, determined, as he wrote in his autobiography, to travel via "the wildest, leafiest, and least trodden way" he could find. His final destination was Florida, but he had no set itinerary. He wended his way south by whatever path took his fancy.

THE WAY TO THE GULF

Muir traveled from Wisconsin to Kentucky, where he would begin his long trek. He traveled light. His small, waterproof rubber sack contained one change of underwear, three of his favorite books (including the New Testament), a few essential toiletries, his plant press, and about $30. On average, Muir walked from 20 to 25 miles (32 to 40 km) per day.

In Kentucky, he met a man who lived near Mammoth Cave. When Muir asked him if the caves were as magnificent as he had heard, the man shrugged. He had never bothered to visit that "hole in the ground." In his writings, Muir assessed this common American attitude that: "one was too wise to waste precious time with weeds, caves, fossils, or anything else that [one] could not eat." This theme would obsess Muir: How could Americans, who are surrounded by a continent filled with marvels and sublime natural beauty "not be touched or even mildly interested in [these] spectacular features. . . . [What] was the reason for this slothful insensitivity?" Muir pondered this aesthetic—some would say spiritual—blindness among his countrymen throughout his life.

Muir walked through the "paradise of oaks" that covered much of Kentucky and entered Tennessee, where he saw his first mountains—the Cumberlands. Muir immediately climbed a peak to view the panorama of these ancient, rolling, and beautifully serene mountains. He then headed southeast toward North Carolina. The few folks he met in the war-ruined town of Jamestown advised him to stock up on food. They said the war had emptied the land of most of its residents, and he'd be hard-pressed to find a bed or a meal until he reached Florida. Their warnings turned out to be true. As he hiked toward Georgia, Muir passed by the scorched ruins of former towns and farms. The Civil War had made a wasteland of this part of the South. Still, on the few occasions when Muir found an inhabited homestead, the farming family always generously shared with Muir what little food they had.

Bandits, or "bushwhackers," were a constant threat, and Muir met up with a few during his travels. Yet, each time he encountered these thieves, they let him go. It was obvious to them that this poor, ragged hiker had nothing of value. Even attempting to rob him would have been a waste of their time.

On September 14, 1867, Muir got his first glimpse of the Great Smoky Mountains. As Muir neared the Smokies, he frequently stopped to breathe the magical mountain air and his soul filled with joy. (Muir's intense reaction to the Smokies was only a foretaste of the profound soul-connection he would later find in the Sierra Nevadas.) The next day, Muir scaled his first major peak and marveled at the breathtaking vistas from the mountaintop. Muir made the following entry in his journal after his first ascent: "Such an

This photo shows a typically stunning view of the Great Smoky Mountains, which became a national park in 1940. Because it is protected as a national park, the land remains largely untouched since the days when John Muir explored the area.

ocean of wooded, waving, swelling mountain beauty and grandeur is not to be described. . . . Oh, these forest gardens of our Father! What perfection, what divinity! . . . Who shall read the teaching of these sylvan pages?" The answer to this question would eventually become clear: It would be John Muir who would witness and then teach others about the presence of God in nature. Even as he wrote those lines in his journal, Muir wondered if the responsibility for relating this divine interpretation to the rest of the world might fall to him.

After exploring the Smokies, Muir continued south along the Hiwassee River into North Carolina. Muir wandered through the red and gold autumn forests that rimmed the river. His route was solitary, wild, and untrodden, with only the river's whooshing and trilling whispers to keep him company. Here, he experienced the deep peace and sublime tranquility he had always found in untouched nature.

As Muir entered Georgia, the landscape changed from forest to open, sandy savanna where entirely new forms of plant life grew.

Muir saw Spanish moss and long-leafed pine for the first time and delighted in eating wild muscadine grapes. The Deep South was a different world from the Midwest, and the farther Muir traveled into it, the stranger it seemed. On October 1, Muir entered his first cypress swamp in the vicinity of the Savannah River. As he slogged through the black swamp waters, with the towering, moss-laden trees blocking out the sun, Muir admitted to feeling "indescribable loneliness."

Muir may have reveled in being one with nature, but he knew that every one of God's creatures acts according to its nature. Muir was no fool, so he kept a sharp lookout for alligators, whose

THE GREAT SMOKY MOUNTAINS

The Smokies are among the oldest mountains in the world, having formed about 200 to 300 million years ago. They are considered to be part of the Appalachian Mountain chain and are unique in that they run northeast to southwest, an orientation that has allowed a great diversity of plants and animals to evolve and thrive in them. During the last ice age, about 10,000 years ago, the orientation of the ranges permitted animals and plants to migrate along the peaks. Because the Smokies were not covered with glaciers, they became a refuge for countless plants and animals. More than 10,000 species of plants and animals are found in the Smokies.

Hundreds of millions of years of weathering has worn down the once jagged and lofty peaks of the Smokies. That is why these ancient mountains have a gentler, more rounded appearance than more recently created mountains, such as the Rockies. Today, the Great Smoky Mountains National Park protects the landscape and its creatures.

God-given nature might induce them to make a meal out of him. Still, Muir understood that alligators were not the "devils" humans thought they were. He believed that alligators, like all creatures, have their important part to play in God's grand scheme. People loathe and fear animals like alligators because they don't understand how they fit into that scheme. His musings on these questions reveal Muir's innate understanding of ecology, which was not yet a recognized science. They also demonstrate Muir's conviction that humans are not and should not consider themselves the "measure of creation." Instead, Muir preferred to take a wider view, believing that humans were one among many forms of life, and each form had a special mission on Earth.

One night, Muir slept in a cemetery where he keenly felt the presence of all the soldiers and civilians who had died during the war. As he contemplated the dead and all the living things he had encountered during his journey, Muir concluded that death and life were part of a cycle. As he wrote in his journal, Muir understood that "life and death were not opposites; they were the same thing. All was process, all was cyclical. . . . Sympathy, the friendly union of life and death [is] so apparent in Nature. We are taught that death is an accident, a deplorable punishment for the oldest sin, the arch-enemy of life, . . . but [if] children walk with Nature [and] see the beautiful blendings and communions of death and life, their inseparable unity, . . . they will learn that death is stingless indeed, and as beautiful as life [because] All is divine harmony." This wisdom was a deep and powerful breakthrough for Muir, who would demonstrate fearlessness in the face of death for the rest of his life.

Muir found that the swamps south of Savannah were impenetrable, so he boarded a schooner to carry him to the Gulf of Mexico. On October 23, 1867, Muir finally saw the vast waters of the Gulf, a sight that made him feel giddy. As he gazed at the distant, watery horizon, his thoughts turned to his own master plan—to ship out from the Gulf for South America where he would spend years exploring the Andes Mountains and the Amazon rain forest.

A great egret stands on the limb of a cypress tree on Caddo Lake, near Uncertain, Texas. This cypress swamp is typical of those in the U.S. Southeast. Cypress trees have wide bases, called buttresses, that help them stay upright in their watery habitat.

The Best-Laid Plans . . .

Muir asked everyone he met if they knew of a boat he could take to get to Cuba. Richard Hodgson, a local sawmill owner, told Muir about a schooner that was scheduled to sail in two weeks with a stopover in Cuba. In the meantime, Hodgson informed him, Muir could earn some extra money working at Hodgson's sawmill. Though Muir was impatient to set out, he agreed.

One day not long after he started work, Muir felt unusually tired while prowling the seashore looking for plants. He went for a swim, thinking it would revive his energies, which he thought might have been depleted during his long trek. The swim, however, left him more fatigued. One afternoon, a few days later, on the way from the sawmill to the hostel where he was staying, Muir suddenly collapsed. He lay on the dirt road, feverish and unconscious, until the middle of the night. When he regained consciousness, he managed to stagger forward a short distance before he collapsed again. He rose, staggered some more, and collapsed over and over again: In the end, it took him until the morning to get to his hostel. Muir begged

MALARIA

Malaria is a terrible, often fatal, disease that is caused by a parasitic microbe that is transmitted to humans via a bite from an infected *Anopheles* mosquito. The parasite, called plasmodium, travels to the infected person's liver, where it grows and multiplies. Then the countless parasites enter the bloodstream where they infect red blood cells. Generations of microbes reproduce in red blood cells, killing them in the process. When the red blood cells die, they release even more parasites into the bloodstream where they infect yet more red blood cells. The disease is transmitted when a mosquito bites and ingests blood from a person who is infected with malaria. When that mosquito then bites an uninfected person, it transmits the parasite in its saliva to the new victim.

The fever, shaking, vomiting, aching, and other symptoms appear when many red blood cells have been destroyed and the malaria parasite is swarming through the body. These symptoms usually begin between 10 to 18 days after a person has been bitten by an infected mosquito.

Malaria kills millions of people around the world every year. It is found in a wide variety of climates, but it is especially prevalent in wetlands, where insect larvae grow and hatch. To date, there is no cure.

the watchman to help him to his bed, but the man thought he was drunk, and ignored him. Muir had to struggle on his own to his bunk, where he finally collapsed.

It is likely that Muir contracted malaria from an infected mosquito while he was slogging through a swamp. The disease struck Muir down like a thunderbolt. Hodgson carried the extremely ill and weak man to his home, where Muir lay unconscious and shaking with fever for days. He was bedridden for three months, and he almost died before the illness abated and he began to regain his strength. In January 1868, he was finally able to rise from his bed and begin tentatively to walk on his own.

When he was able to leave the house, Muir spent most of his time sitting in the shade of oak trees, looking out over the Gulf. He sketched a few birds and plants. Most of the time, though, he contemplated the water while waiting for his strength to return. Finally, one day, out of the blue, Muir felt an irresistible urge to pick up his journal and write.

THE RELIGION OF NATURE

Muir wrote down his ideas about religion and nature. Perhaps it was his brush with death that confirmed him in his views of religion. Whatever the case, Muir wrote with conviction and power.

In his journal, Muir wrote: "The world, we are told, was made especially for man, a presumption not supported by all the facts. . . . This star, our own good earth, made many a successful journey around the heavens ere man was made, and whole kingdoms of creatures enjoyed existence and returned to dust ere man appeared to claim them. After human beings have also played their part in Creation's plan, they too may disappear without any . . . extraordinary commotion whatever."

What Muir most deplored was humanity's notion that it was the center of the universe and that God had created the universe solely for human use. This, Muir believed, is a notion taught by orthodox Christianity. Such notions led to the presumption that creation and nature should be valued only insofar as they are useful to humans. As self-proclaimed lords over the Earth, people believed that God had made sheep just so humans could have wool and mutton, for example. It follows that all parts of creation that are not useful to humans are dismissed, ignored, or said to be evil. The orthodox Christian view that it was only humans who were possessed of a soul was equally offensive to Muir. About this Muir wrote, "Plants are credited with but a dim and uncertain sensation and minerals with positively none at all. But why may not even a mineral arrangement of matter be endowed with sensation of a kind [or a soul] . . . that we in our blind exclusive perfection can have no manner of communication with?" Plants and rocks, like us, are integral parts of God's creation. By what right do we deny them their share of God's spirit and honor them as being as much a manifestation of God as we are?

In the biography *John Muir: Rediscovering America,* author Frederick Turner describes Muir's belief this way: "[H]ow could you truly contemplate the phenomena of the natural world *without* believing that all things had their germane purposes and their own deep lives to lead? . . . It was more likely that [all of creation is] equal in the eye of the Creator and has an essential part to play in [God's] master plan. . . . [Therefore] Nature was all you needed to know of God." For Muir, this was the essential teaching of Christ and the way for humans to come to God.

Muir lived by and wrote about these mature and profound religious ideas for the rest of his life. He never ceased to see God in every aspect or part of creation, no matter how minute or irrelevant it seemed to the common run of humanity.

CALIFORNIA

Muir continued to search for a ship that would take him to South America. Unfortunately, he could not shake the weakness that remained from his bout with malaria. He realized that, in his weakened condition, he would have to abandon his dreams of exotic exploration. So, he thought, if he couldn't sail south, he would head north instead. He sailed north to New York City to find another vessel to get him to California. In February 1868, Muir boarded the schooner *Island Belle* and sailed south to the isthmus of Central America (which he crossed by train, as the Panama Canal was not yet built) and then took a boat up the West Coast to California.

Muir had no precise destination in mind. While working in Indianapolis, he had heard talk of a place called Yosemite, so he thought he might go there. On March 17, Muir sailed into San Francisco harbor.

6

Muir's Life's Work and His Soul's Ecstasy

THE SIERRA

John Muir took no notice of the lovely city of San Francisco. Legend has it that as soon as he debarked from his ship, he asked directions for the quickest way out of town and into the mountains. He fled the city, determined to set his eyes on the Sierra Nevada Mountains. It was April 1868, and every landscape he crossed was painted with the colors of millions of wildflowers. Muir describes himself as experiencing a "vast capacity for happiness" as he walked through this enchanted land.

At the top of Pacheco Pass, east of the city of San Jose, Muir saw the Sierra Nevada for the first time. Although he was 100 miles (161 km) away from the range, he marveled at its endless undulations that stretched out before him as far as the eye could see. The joy he felt was intensified by the exquisite sight of the miles of "deep, glowing masses" of wildflowers that blanketed the entire San Joaquin Valley below. Finding the sight irresistible, Muir made for the valley, where he waded through the endless, waving fields of color.

The Sierra Nevada Mountains stretch through California and Nevada for 400 miles (643.7 km) from north to south. The Sierra Nevada area includes Yosemite, Sequoia, and Kings Canyon national parks.

Eventually, it came time for Muir to restock his provisions, so he left "paradise" and stopped in the tiny mining town of Coulterville in the Sierra foothills, where he bought flour, crackers, and other items at Bruschi's general store. Muir was perfectly content to live on a diet of "bread and water" so long as he could eat it while wandering in his beloved wilderness. As he headed back toward the peaks, Muir passed through Mariposa Grove, where he saw giant sequoias for the first time. Muir was so humbled by the sight, he felt unworthy even to set eyes on the huge, magnificent trees.

The Shepherd

After a few weeks among the redwoods, Muir needed to buy more provisions. Once again, it was time to head back to "civilization" to earn enough money so he could continue to live in the mountains for

THE WORLD'S TALLEST TREES

The giant sequoias of Northern California are a type of redwood tree. Sequoias and redwoods are the tallest trees in the world. Giant sequoias typically grow to a height of 325 feet (99 m), while redwoods can reach 385 feet (117 m). Many of these slow-growing sequoias are 3,000 to 4,000 years old. The trunks of sequoias and redwoods range from 10 to 30 feet (3 to 9 m) in diameter.

Though the U.S. government protects some of the last remnants of these forests—in Sequoia National Park and Redwood National Park—the deep, red wood of these trees is highly valued for its resistance to the elements. Even today, homes are built with outdoor decks or hot tubs that are made out of redwood.

Sequoia National Park is located in the southern Sierra Nevada. The park is famous for its giant sequoia trees, including one called "General Sherman," which is the largest tree on Earth at 275 feet (84 meters) tall.

an extended period. In August 1868, Muir got a dilapidated and filthy room at "Smoky" Jack's hostel in a nearly abandoned mining town. Despite the hostel's soot-covered walls and leaky roof, Muir refused to feel sorry for himself. He was determined to make creative use of the wintertime to make plans for the future. He got a job as a shepherd, but spent as much time as he could sketching plants and animals and recording the changes he saw in nature as the seasons changed. In December, the rains came and. through the first months of 1869, Muir recorded the rebirth of life that the welcome rain brought to the land. While Muir studied changes in the land, he tended the sheep as best he could. Still, about 100 sheep died of the cold and wet during February. Muir lamented that "Man has injured every animal he has touched . . . [even] these poor unfriended creatures."

The lush explosion of life and color Muir had seen in March turned burnt gold by June when the dry season came and parched the land. By this time, Muir had gotten a job as an overseer of shepherds for Pat Delaney, who owned a large flock of sheep. Delaney was intrigued by Muir and his eccentric interest in plants and animals. By hiring Muir as an overseer instead of a sheepherder, Delaney made sure that Muir had few responsibilities during the day and thus could dedicate most of his time to observing nature, sketching, and writing in his journal. This job turned out to be a godsend for Muir.

The Epiphany

Muir and the shepherds guided the herd up toward the alpine meadows, where the murderous heat and dryness had not killed the vegetation that would fatten the animals. After six days of uphill trekking, Muir entered the true alpine environment, with its majestic trees and magnificent vistas. Muir notes again in his writings the sense of ecstasy that he felt: "We are now in the mountains and they are in us . . . making every nerve quiver, filling every pore and cell of us. . . . [My body] seems as transparent as glass to the beauty . . . [and] an inseparable part of it."

From his vantage point high in the Sierra, Muir glimpsed the towering snow-covered peaks of Yosemite. It was a pivotal moment in Muir's life. In one moment of perfect clarity, Muir saw that all his previous experiences—in Canada and while hiking to Florida—had been preparation for his arrival in this place. He realized it was his destiny and knew he had made exactly the right choice in coming to the Sierra Nevada Mountains.

Becoming one with Yosemite became his life's calling, even if Muir did not yet understand exactly what that meant or how exactly he would accomplish it. What he did know was that his life would not be a practical one that would make him rich, except in spirit. And that was fine with him. In a letter to his sister Sarah, he wrote:

> I know that I could under ordinary circumstances accumulate wealth and obtain a fair position in society, and I am arrived at an age that requires that I should choose some definite course for life. . . . [But] I am captive. I am bound. Love of pure unblemished Nature seems to overmaster and blur out of sight all other objects and considerations. . . . [I shall live] among the sublimities of Yosemite and forget that ever a thought of civilization or time-honored proprieties came among my pathless, lawless thoughts and wanderings.

For the rest of that summer of 1869, while the shepherds he supervised tended the flocks, Muir deported himself like a carefree schoolboy. He slept out on rocks in the middle of streams or hidden among the tall wildflowers in alpine meadows. Whenever the whim hit him, he climbed trees and savored the view from the treetops. Muir was fancy-free and in his element.

ABSORBING NATURE

Despite his ecstasy at finding his life's calling in nature, Muir also recognized that he faced a dilemma. Yosemite was so monumental and so overwhelming, how could he ever come to fully understand and become one with it? Where does a person begin to understand an environment on such a huge scale, one that is so overwhelmingly huge and spectacularly beautiful?

Muir decided that the only reasonable way to approach his beloved Yosemite was to observe it intimately; by beginning at the smallest scale and then gradually to expand the scale of his observations until they encompassed the entire landscape. In this way, too, he would come to understand not only the individual parts of the terrain but how all the living and non-living things in the landscape fit and functioned together.

Muir began by carefully observing the lives of ants and other insects. He examined the tiniest mosses and then the larger plants that shaded them. He studied and sketched animal tracks and followed them as far as he could to see what they revealed about the lives of the animals that made Yosemite their home. As he moved from place to place and from low to high elevations, he noted how the environment changed and how each environment was home to its own community of plants and animals. As a botanist, he studied the enormous diversity of plant life throughout Yosemite. The more closely and completely he observed living things, the more they revealed their innermost nature to him. Muir came to understand the intimate and harmonious interactions among things that breathe such glorious life into the natural world.

Muir wrote in his journal that when looking at any one thing in nature "we find it hitched to everything else in the universe. . . . [I learned] the lessons of unity and the interrelation of all the features of the landscape revealed in general views." Though he did not know it, by the end of his first summer in Yosemite, Muir was expressing ideas that would become the foundation of the science of ecology.

When the first frosts settled on the mountains, Muir and the other shepherds led the flocks back down into the valley. In earlier times, Muir might have become despondent at the prospect of wintering in "civilization." Not now. Muir returned filled with the conviction that he had found his way in life. He no longer worried that he would end up living the life of "quiet desperation" that fellow-nature lover and writer Henry David Thoreau observed among most people. Muir wrote that he foresaw a "good time coming, when money enough will be earned to enable me to go walking where I like in pure wildness, with what I can carry on my back, and when the bread-sack is empty, run down to the nearest bread-line for more."

THE WILDERNESS YEARS

After delivering Delaney's sheep, Muir used some of his earnings to buy the bare necessities (such as crackers and tea) and, in November 1869, he returned to Yosemite. With brief breaks for work and re-provisioning, he spent almost all of the next five years living in and becoming one with this wilderness that he loved so much. This five-year period shaped the core of Muir's being and was the time of his greatest intellectual and spiritual growth.

Nothing could stop him now. Even camping out in the chill of winter was a delight for Muir, who wrote to Jeanne Carr that "I am dead and gone to heaven." In a way, Muir was dead to the world of ordinary people and civilized life, but he lived in a perpetual, though solitary, bliss that opened and deepened his soul.

During these years, Muir was determined to know and experience every aspect of nature. He was so attuned to its rhythms and so comfortable with the concept of death as part of life that he often achieved feats of astounding physical strength and bravery. He climbed sheer vertical rock faces without ropes or other aids, sometimes nearly dying in the process. Yet the fear of death had no hold over him. Climbing mountains in the depths of winter he was often forced to sleep out on exposed rock ledges without even the comfort of a blanket, which he felt hampered his rock climbing. He awoke (if he had slept at all) half-frozen and aching, but a small fire, a cup of hot tea, and the warming sun always revived him.

One particularly famous incident, however, made some people question (mistakenly) Muir's sense of self-preservation. In December 1874, a huge thunderstorm rolled over the mountains, but instead of seeking shelter, Muir climbed up to the highest wooded peak he could reach. Then he climbed to the very top of the tallest tree he found there. He wanted to experience a storm the way a tree experiences it. Muir later published an account of this experience:

I experienced no difficulty in reaching the top of this [100-foot-tall; 30 m] tree, and never before did I enjoy so noble an exhilaration of motion. The slender top fairly flapped and swished in the passionate torrent, bending and swirling backward and forward round and round, tracing indescribable combinations of vertical and horizontal curves, while I clung with muscles firm braced, like a bobolink on a reed. . . . [I] was free to take the wind into my pulses and enjoy the excited forest from my superb outlook. . . . The sounds of the storm corresponded gloriously with the wild exuberance of light and motion. The profound bass of the naked branches and boles booming like waterfalls; the quick, tense vibrations of the pine needles, now rising to a shrill, whistling hiss, now falling to a silky murmur; the rustling of laurel groves in the dells, and the keen metallic click of leaf on leaf—all this was heard in easy analysis when the attention was calmly bent. . . . I kept my lofty perch for hours, frequently closing my eyes to enjoy the music by itself. . . . When the storm began to abate, I dismounted and sauntered down through the calming woods. . . . The setting sun . . . seemed to say 'My peace I give unto you.'

This experience provides some idea of the lengths to which Muir would go to fully experience and become one with the landscape and its living things. In one of his letters to Jeanne Carr, written in 1870, he describes himself as "rich beyond measure."

Forms and Forces

As he gained greater oneness with the life of Yosemite, Muir began to wonder what forces of nature had shaped its glorious peaks and valleys. The botanist turned his scientific curiosity and intellect toward discovering the geological forces that created such splendor.

Around that time, a team of scientists with the U.S. Geological Survey had come to Yosemite to find out what geological forces had created its spectacular environment. Geologists on an 1863 survey found features that they believed showed that Yosemite Valley had been shaped by glaciers. However, most geologists back then thought that Yosemite's peaks had been created through violent uplift of the Earth's crust, while Yosemite Valley had been formed by a sudden and massive sinking of the valley floor. Muir did not have an axe to grind in this argument. He simply wanted to find out how Yosemite was created.

Muir had explored virtually every inch of Yosemite and had noted distinct signs of previous glaciation. Remember that although Muir was a naturalist, he had been trained in geology at college. Muir noted the obvious gouges and deep markings in the valley that are the hallmarks of a huge glacier grinding over bedrock. These and other features convinced Muir that Yosemite had been shaped by glaciation. He described his findings and conclusions in letters to Jeanne and Professor Carr. The Carrs related Muir's ideas and evidence to well-known geologists of their acquaintance. By the early 1870s, some of these geologists traveled to California to meet Muir and see the evidence for themselves. In 1870, Joseph Le Conte, a geologist with the University of California, visited Muir and was impressed by his evidence. Le Conte later wrote that Muir was a man "of rare intelligence [and] of much knowledge of science."

A year later, John D. Runkle, president of the Massachusetts Institute of Technology, traversed the continent to spend five days with Muir in Yosemite. At the end of his visit, Runkle was also convinced of the glaciation theory. Then, in October 1871, Muir located a living glacier on Red Mountain, in the Merced group near Yosemite. He had found solid scientific evidence that glaciers occurred in and formed Yosemite.

While Muir knew that he had made a notable geological discovery, he remained satisfied to simply jot down his findings in his journal. Jeanne Carr, however, insisted that Muir owed it to both himself and the world to publish the results of his research. She strongly felt that Muir's deep insights—both scientific and spiritual— revealed what an extraordinary man John Muir was. Yet Muir was extremely reluctant to publish, as he feared that once he became known to the "civilized" world, his blissful sojourn in Yosemite would be over.

GLACIATION IN YOSEMITE

Today, there is no doubt that Yosemite was formed by glaciers. As early as 1.2 million years ago, glaciers covered the Yosemite region. The ancient, 1,000-foot-deep (304.8 m) glaciers carved out Yosemite Valley as they ground their way through deep, narrow canyons, where rivers formed in their wake. The weight and gouging motion of the glaciers created the wide, U-shaped canyons and valleys found in Yosemite today. However, in some parts of Yosemite, the massive sheets of ice merely polished the rocky surface, leaving towers of rock standing within the valleys.

About 30,000 years ago, Yosemite was again covered in ice from what is called the Tioga Glaciation. Ice covered most of Yosemite for a period of about 20,000 years. As the glacier retreated, its terminal moraine (deposits of rock and debris left behind by the melting glacier) dammed one valley and led to the formation of Lake Yosemite. Over time, sediment filled Yosemite's valleys completely.

Lyell glacier is one of the few remaining glaciers in Yosemite National Park.

In some ways, these fears were justified. Finally though, Muir gave in to the pressure from Jeanne Carr and wrote an article titled "Yosemite Glaciers" that was published in the *New York Tribune* on December 5, 1871. The paper paid him $200 for the piece, in which he wrote:

> I have been drifting about among the rocks of this region for several years, anxious to spell out some of the mountain truths which are written here. . . . There is a sublimity in the life of a glacier . . . [which] exert[s] tremendous energies in silence and darkness, outspread, spirit-like, brooding above predestined rocks unknown to light, unborn, working on un-wearied through unmeasured time . . . until at length, their creations complete, their mountains brought forth, homes made for the meadows and lakes, and fields for waiting forests, . . . they depart.

Muir's article was no ordinary, dry-as-dust scientific research report. It revealed to the public that Muir was a deeply poetic and spiritual soul as well as a man of science. The positive response to this essay led the *Tribune* to ask for more articles. Muir's apprehensions were being realized: As the world took notice of him, Muir's life and his world would change.

Resistance
and Return

The 1870s were a time of inner conflict and turmoil for John Muir. He was torn between his craving to disappear into the wilderness and live forever in ecstatic solitude and the growing demand that he share his experiences with the world through his writing. Though today Muir is considered one of America's greatest nature writers, he found writing an excruciating and almost futile exercise. "It was easy to enjoy nature," he noted, "It is not easy to tell about it . . . One's feelings are always in advance of words, so much is deeply felt that is in its very nature undefinable . . . [T]here is some infinite shortcoming. . . . The few hard words make but a skeleton, fleshless, heartless, and when you read, the dead bony words rattle in one's teeth."

To make matters worse, Muir found he could not write for publication while he was living in the wilderness. He felt that this was in some way a desecration of nature and that the landscape was rejecting both him and his writing. Therefore, in order for him to write for publication, he had to come down from his beloved mountains and rejoin society.

Muir was also troubled by Jeanne Carr's insistence that he leave the wilderness permanently and become a writer. Carr had always been Muir's guiding light, and to a great extent, he was most grateful to her for encouraging him to find his true calling in nature. Now, here she was demanding that he give up living in the wild and instead dedicate himself to seeking fame and fortune. In some ways, Muir felt betrayed by his best friend. Yet, he also felt that he owed her a huge debt of gratitude. Jeanne Carr was much in Muir's thoughts as he debated with himself about what he should do.

It was Carr who arranged Muir's meeting with Ralph Waldo Emerson, the renowned transcendentalist, whose writings about the value of wild nature had been an inspiration for Muir. Emerson knew the Carrs, who had moved to Oakland, California. When Emerson visited them in 1871, Jeanne urged him to tour Yosemite with Muir. Emerson was delighted by the idea, while Muir was thrilled at the idea of meeting one of his heroes. The two men liked each other instantly. However, Muir was disappointed that Emerson would not go on a camping trip with him. Instead, Emerson took only day trips into Yosemite with Muir and spent his nights at a nearby lodge. Emerson was 68 years old then, and his entourage of admirers and assistants refused to allow the great man to risk his health by sleeping outdoors. Still, Emerson was greatly impressed by Muir's spirit and love of nature as well as by his extensive knowledge of the botany and geology of the area.

In an 1872 letter to Muir, Emerson made the mountain man a remarkable offer. He suggested that Muir come to live at his home in Concord, Massachusetts, where he would meet other great men of science. Muir was flattered to get such a rare and generous invitation, but he was adamant that he would remain in the mountains. In homage to Emerson, Muir reread some of the great man's essays. Among the many passages he marked were those in which Emerson explained why it was necessary for the man of nature to share his understanding and knowledge with the world. Emerson applauded the impulse to become one with nature, but he also argued that the person who achieved that oneness had an obligation to act in the world. The person who had experienced the truth had to share the truth with others.

Muir again felt pressured about what he should do. Emerson and Carr urged him to give up his freedom and return to civilization

Ralph Waldo Emerson was 68 when he met 33-year-old John Muir, and he greatly influenced the younger man's writing.

RALPH WALDO EMERSON AND TRANSCENDENTALISM

Ralph Waldo Emerson (1803–1882) was one of the most influential and respected thinkers and writers of his age. Emerson was a Boston-born, Harvard-educated intellectual who had traveled to Europe in his youth and been strongly influenced by the mystical ideas of Romantic philosophers, such as the poet William Wordsworth. In his 1836 book *Nature,* Emerson set out the main principles of transcendentalism, a movement that he led along with Henry David Thoreau. Transcendentalism is a philosophy that emphasizes the spiritual unity of all nature, or creation. Emerson wrote and lectured widely, teaching that there are ways of knowing and being that are beyond everyday experience and the rational mind. Immersing oneself in nature was the way that humans could touch and understand those aspects of reality that are beyond rationality and ordinary experience.

to write about the truths his remarkable life had taught him. Muir resisted their pressure as best he could. He still had a strong desire to remain in the wilderness. For most of 1872 and 1873, he remained a mountain man, with brief stints helping run a tourist lodge and working as a guide for tourists visiting Yosemite. As always, as soon as he earned enough money for supplies, he returned to his mountain solitude.

Throughout this period, the fierce tug-of-war between Carr and Muir continued. In her letters to Muir, Carr begged him to return to society. In his letters to Carr, Muir waxed ecstatic about his oneness with nature. In one letter, he wrote, "I feel sure that if you were here to see how happy I am . . . you would not call me away."

Nevertheless, Carr persisted. In 1872, she wrote Muir that she had already made plans for him to come and live with her family in Oakland where he could become the successful man of letters he deserved to be. Instead of going to Oakland, however, Muir disappeared further into the wilderness, toward the Tuolumne River, the Hetch Hetchy Valley, and the summit of Mount Ritter.

Several months later, Muir finally paid Carr a visit in Oakland. He was horrified at the crowds, noise, and confusion of city life and immediately fled back into the mountains. Yet this visit marked a turning point in Muir's life. By 1873, he began to realize that perhaps his days of natural solitude were over. The few essays of his that had been published had attracted a wide and admiring audience. Perhaps, Muir thought, he should start to share more of his experience with the public. Muir had always thought that ordinary people would never be receptive to, or understand, what he had to say. Yet he began to realize that, at least for some people, his writings about the divinity of nature struck a deep chord. Maybe, he thought, his writings could sway people to value nature the way he did. Muir held out in his mountain solitude until 1874, at which time he decided to return to civilization.

NOVICE WRITER

Muir had to begin his public writing career to fulfill a publishing contract. He worked through the spring of 1873 on essays about his experiences in the Sierra. However, when summer came, he escaped into the mountains. That autumn, he traveled to Oakland to live with friends, the McChesneys.

Muir labored on his wilderness essays, finding them, as usual, a torment to write. He also found being confined indoors in his room almost unbearable. In May 1873, the first of his Sierra essays appeared in the *Overland Monthly*. Every month, Muir sent in another essay until, in January 1874, the Sierra series was complete. His contract fulfilled, Muir rushed out of the city and back to his beloved mountains. How wonderful it was to feel the

31

The Sabbath.

With grateful toil and cares opprest-,
The Christian day brings welcome rest--
'Mong giant oaks, their trembling house
Shrinks cowering like a mountain mouse,-
Unpacked, their books and plants around
Are sprinkled on the breezy ground,
While all intent on heavenly things,
They seek the bliss which Sabbath brings.
All nature now is calmly gay,
And seems to know 'tis Sabbath day,
These glowing hours of holy calm
Are laden with a richer balm-
More softly treads the morning breeze
Its leafy path of arching trees-
Less noisy now the fearless rill-
A smoother haze is on the hill;
And sounds come all in harmony
With will of holy melody.

Their hearts are swayed with reverent fear,
As heavenly footsteps come more near,
And kneeling on the grassy sod,
Their hearts in prayer ascend to God.

One reads aloud the sacred page
How Love divine from age to age,
Hath marked mankind with pitying eye,
And spared a race condemned to die.
And how the Saviour left the skies-
How stooped so low that man may rise-
Of love unstained to all his foes,
What tears he shed for others woes;

John Muir was an avid writer—in his journal, in letters to friends,
and in articles for the general public. This is a page of Muir's writing on the subject of "The Sabbath."

living earth, instead of hard pavement, beneath his feet. As soon as he entered the wilderness, the fatigue and weakness he had felt in the city lifted. The joy of freedom filled his soul once again. The farther he traveled into the wilderness, the more deadly and poisonous civilization seemed to him. Tellingly, in his journal, he compared city living with his near-death experience digging the well at his family's Hickory Hill farm. Both places were, he felt, equally suffocating.

Yet something had changed. Muir noted sadly that "None of the rocks seems to call me now . . . Surely this . . . chapter of my life is over." Muir continued to wander the wilds through 1874, heading farther into Northern California to climb Mount Shasta. (It was during this trip that Muir had his amazing tree-top experience of a violent storm.) Still, Muir wrote in a letter to Carr that he felt "a sort of nervous fear of another period of town dark" approaching for him.

In early 1875, Muir returned to Oakland where he lived with some other friends, the Swetts. From this point onward, the time of living his life wholly immersed in nature was over for Muir. From now on, he would divide his time between civilization and the wilderness. Muir wrote a letter to his sister saying, "I have not yet in all my wanderings found a single person so free as myself . . . [Yet now] I am bound to the laws of my own life . . . I am swept onward in a general current that bears on irresistibly." Muir spent the spring of 1875 writing his essay "Wild Wool," which was published in the *Overland Monthly*. Muir intended the essay to entice civilized people to appreciate wild nature's beauty, grandeur, and inherent value. And it did just that.

THE PURSUIT OF MONEY AND THE LOSS OF THE AMERICAN SOUL

Muir spent the summer of 1874 in the Sierra where, his journal reveals, he thought a great deal about the relationship between wilderness and society. He worried about the effects of human activity on nature and wilderness. As he noted in his journal, "What

[will] man do with the mountains? . . . Will he cut down all the trees to make ships and houses? . . . What is the human part [in] the mountains' destiny?" Already, Muir was seeing the intrusion of human activity into areas that had been untouched wilderness only a few years before. Forests were being felled for lumber, mountains were being scarred by mines, and even the stupendous sequoias were being sacrificed to commercial interests that saw them not in terms of ancient and magnificent works of nature but in terms of the number of board-feet of timber they contained.

In January 1876, Muir gave his first public lecture about nature at the Literary Institute of Sacramento. That winter, Muir produced more essays. One of them, "God's First Temples: How Shall We Preserve Our Forests?" an argument for conservation and against deforestation, was published in the Sacramento *Record-Union*. In this and later essays, Muir addresses the destiny of the American wilderness in the face of economic development. Since the close of the Civil War, the United States—once called "Nature's nation"—had turned all its energies toward exploiting the continent's natural resources for economic gain. Where would that end? Muir asked. Would all the country's wilderness be destroyed in the name of "progress?"

The year 1876 was the nation's centennial, and a huge celebration was held in Philadelphia. It was clear that what the nation celebrated on its 100th birthday was not the wild beauty it contained but the invention of machines that helped people destroy that beauty for profit. The nation, it seemed, valued money above all things, and all things were to be sacrificed to the greed for it.

As Muir walked the streets of Oakland and San Francisco, he despaired at the mindless sprawl of the city and of the way it cut people off from the natural world, both physically and mentally. People were so detached from nature, no one seemed to care what happened to it. That is why they could act so thoughtlessly in destroying it. Muir diagnosed the moral and spiritual emptiness of Americans as "hollowness at heart." "Heaven help you all" was Muir's despairing response to the destruction he saw spreading through the land, and to the narrow, unnatural city life most people lived.

Gold Hill, Nevada, is one of many ghost towns from the mining era of the late 1800s. Such towns sprung up when ore was discovered, but were quickly abandoned if a richer collection of ore was found elsewhere.

Muir spent the summer of 1877 traveling through Utah and Nevada. He wrote of these travels for the San Francisco *Evening Bulletin*, describing the vast landscapes plundered by miners: "[The region] was already strewn with ruins that seem as gray and silent and time-worn as if the civilization to which they belonged had perished centuries ago" instead of just decades ago. Everywhere, the "dead mining towns" bore witness to people's insatiable search for riches. Landscape after landscape was scraped raw for its ore and then left as dead as a moonscape. The widespread destruction was, for Muir, evidence that wealth-seekers ravaged the land "blindly like raving madmen" whose prayers for riches could never be answered because they were "not in harmony with nature."

ENGAGEMENT AND ESCAPE

In addition to his literary work during his explorations of the Southwest, Muir also wrote letters to the Strentzels, new friends he had made in Martinez, California. Muir had been introduced to them by their mutual friend, Jeanne Carr. Carr had written the Strentzels about Muir and told them how much they would like him. However, she had an ulterior motive in writing her letters. Earlier, in 1872, Carr wrote to the Strentzels' daughter Louie. This letter reveals how possessive Carr was of Muir. In it, she confesses that "I want you to know my John Muir. . . . I wish I could give him to some noble young woman 'for keeps' and so take him out of the wilderness and into the society of his peers." Jeanne Carr was playing matchmaker to lure Muir out of the wilderness and into society, where she felt he belonged.

By 1878, Muir and the Strentzels had become fast friends. Muir was 40 years old. Louie Strentzel was 31. Both were long past the age at which most people of that time got married. After his 1877 trip to the Southwest, Muir began to court Louie in earnest. Louie was very reserved and old-fashioned, but she was a good match for Muir because he loved to talk and she was a good listener. There are no letters or other records of their courtship or of what they thought of one another. It is likely, though, that Muir saw in Louie the strong and independent woman that lay behind her quiet and retiring outward behavior. In early June 1879, Muir visited the Strentzels and formally asked for Louie's hand in marriage. She accepted and her family approved. Muir was now officially engaged to be married.

Before the engagement was announced, Muir made sure that Louie accepted his plans to travel to Alaska before the wedding. It was a strange request, but Louie agreed to it. Instead of spending glorious love-struck weeks with her betrothed, Louie spent months on her own while her husband-to-be wandered the far north. The separation was a trial for Louie, and in her letters to Muir she wrote of feeling lonely and abandoned. Yet, over the years, Louie would come to understand her husband's need for wilderness and solitude, and she would encourage him to escape whenever he needed to do so.

The First Trip to Alaska

In July 1879, with nary a thought for his fiancée, Muir boarded a ship in Portland, Oregon. He wrote in his journal, "I'm going home.

SEWARD'S FOLLY

William H. Seward was secretary of state under U.S. presidents Lincoln and Johnson. He was a committed expansionist who wanted to see the United States control as much North American land as possible. Until the 1860s, Russia owned the remote, barren, cold, and seemingly useless expanse that would be called Alaska. For years, Russia refused Seward's offer to buy the region. However, after Russia's defeat by the British in the Crimean War (1853–1856), the country feared that the British would take Alaska by force. So, in 1867, when Seward again approached Russia about the sale, it agreed to negotiate. On March 30, 1867, an agreement was signed that transferred ownership of Alaska from Russia to the United States. The U.S. Treasury paid $7.2 million for 586,412 square miles (943,739 square km) of land—an astounding bargain at about two cents per acre.

The treaty of sale was ratified by the Senate, although many in government, the press, and the public were outraged by the deal, which was called "Seward's folly" or "Seward's icebox." Why would the U.S. government spend millions of dollars to buy a frozen wasteland that was not even connected to the lower 48 states? Seward was certain, however, that Alaska would prove to have value; in any case, gaining territory was always a good thing in his view. The United States decided to give the territory the native Aleut name of Alaska. On October 18, 1867, at Sitka, Alaska, the Russian flag came down and the American flag was hoisted in front of the governor's house. Alaska has since proved to be a source of minerals and oil, as well as a jewel of unspoiled American wilderness.

. . . [to] the snow and ice and forests of the north coast." Muir also wrote that for someone who loved wilderness as much as he did, there was no more magical place than the wilds of Alaska.

Muir's ship docked at Fort Wrangell, Alaska, where he soon became friends with the Christian missionary S. Hall Young. In his first rambles around Wrangell and Sitka, Muir saw that some parts of Alaska were no longer the unspoiled wilderness he had expected. In areas where "civilized" people were already living, the destruction of the environment was plain to see, with settlements and the inevitable deforestation that accompanies them. Muir headed away from the settled areas as fast as his legs could carry him. Sometimes accompanied by Young, Muir climbed mountains, delighted in alpine meadows, and paddled up and down rivers that flowed into the wilderness.

For Muir, the best part of the journey was his 800-mile (1,287.4-km) canoe trip to Glacier Bay. Muir was ecstatic. The fog-shrouded bay was rimmed by mountains whose glaciers dipped right down into the water. It was October 1879, and the Alaska winter was quickly approaching, but Muir spent as much time as he could exploring and studying the glaciers and adding to his understanding of how they shaped the landscape.

Wedding Bells

By late November 1879, winter was closing in and it was time to return to Fort Wrangell and head home. At Wrangell, Muir finally collected all the letters that Louie had written to him while he was away. She had pleaded with him to come home soon because she missed him so much. Muir boarded a southbound ship that reached Portland in January 1880. Amazingly, Muir wrote to her from Portland to tell her that he had a few "stops" to make before coming home. The first stop involved giving a few lectures in Portland and a stopover in San Francisco to settle some other "business." It was not until late February 1880 that Muir finally showed up in Martinez and embraced his fiancée for the first time in many months.

The couple was wed on April 14, 1880. They moved into Louie's parents' large house, set amid the thousands of acres of fruit orchards owned by the Strentzels. The elder Strentzels later built a Victorian mansion for themselves a short distance away. It was decided that Muir would take over the running of the huge and highly profitable orchards, as Mr. Strentzel was eager to retire.

The wedding was a small affair, with the Carrs and other friends in attendance. After the ceremony, Muir moved into the first home he had known since leaving Hickory Hill so many years before. As in Wisconsin, he would turn his energies once more to farming.

Writer and Preservationist

(FEELING) DOWN ON THE FARM

John Muir was not a "half-way" type of person. When he focused his mind and energy on something, he put his whole heart, body, and soul into it. So it was with tremendous energy and single-mindedness that Muir took on the job of improving the fruit orchards he had been given to manage. The orchards had been profitable under the elder Strentzel's management, but with Muir at the helm, the 2,600 acres (1,052 ha) of fruit trees bore more fruit—both literally and monetarily—than anyone could have imagined possible.

Muir studied fruit-growing and the growing of grapes for wine (known as viniculture), and he applied his knowledge to improving both the varieties and yields of his orchards. Soon, he was producing crops of the best-quality cherries, pears, apricots, and wine grapes in the region. Following the birth of his two daughters (Wanda in 1881 and Helen in 1886), Muir became obsessed with making money. Now that he had the additional responsibility of supporting a family, Muir felt driven to make as much money as possible. As with most of his endeavors, Muir was wildly successful, and in just a few

Muir's children, Helen and Wanda, pose in this photograph taken around 1888.

years he was rich. The hired hands who worked beside him had a hard time keeping up with their boss, but Muir was a fair and well-liked employer. Among the few things he would not tolerate were laziness and cruelty. Any worker caught overworking or mistreating a farm animal was fired on the spot.

Despite his financial success, a life restricted to farming and moneymaking ate away at Muir. Inside him was the gnawing certainty that he was wasting the precious days of his life doing trivial and mundane tasks. He was confining himself to the demeaning pursuit of wealth while the glories of nature were out there waiting for him. Denying his yearning for the wild took its toll on Muir. His health suffered: his nerves were shot and he suffered from stomach problems and a persistent cough.

In 1888, S. Hall Young, his old missionary friend from Alaska, came to visit. The two men enjoyed reminiscing about their earlier adventures, but Muir became upset when Young said he had left Alaska for good. Muir could not understand how anyone could turn his back on life in such a magnificent setting. However, Muir realized that he, too, had turned his back on the very same way of life. Who was he to criticize his friend when he had done exactly the same thing—giving up the grandeur of the wild in order to raise fruit? Muir's spirits sank and his physical ailments worsened. Young later quoted Muir as lamenting, "I am losing precious days. I am degenerating into a machine for making money. I am learning nothing in this trivial world of men. I must break away and get out into the mountains to learn the news."

WRITING FOR NATURE

Louie Muir could no longer bear to see her husband suffering. She was a wise and understanding woman. Though she would miss him, and though the orchards would have to be managed by someone else for a while, Louie insisted that Muir take time off and go into the wilderness. His sanity and his health depended on it. Muir arranged to travel with a friend to the great forests of Washington and Oregon. After a week or two communing with the Northwest's ancient trees, Muir's health problems vanished. He was in his element again, and he was as happy and carefree as a schoolboy on holiday.

While in Oregon, Muir received a remarkable and insightful letter from Louie. Louie wrote that she recognized how much Muir sacrificed by managing the orchards when his destiny was in nature and his talent was writing about it. She told Muir that nothing should stand in the way of his true calling as a nature writer. He must abandon orchard management and become the writer he was intended to be. The letter lit a spark in Muir. He immediately began writing in his journal about his experiences climbing Mount Rainier and hiking through the Northwest.

The old-growth forests of Oregon made a deep impression on Muir. He again experienced the old ecstasy in his oneness with the great and ancient trees, particularly the magnificent sugar pines. Yet he could not ignore the rate at which these primeval forests were being destroyed for their lumber. As he pondered the American penchant for using the wilderness for commercial means, Muir wrote articles encouraging the creation of a preserve to save some of Oregon's forests.

OPPORTUNITY

In May 1889, Muir met New York City magazine editor Robert Underwood Johnson in a San Francisco hotel. Johnson, the editor of the popular and respected *Century* magazine, did not know what to expect. He knew only that Muir was, by now, something of a national legend. Johnson wanted Muir to write for his magazine. When the two men sat down to dinner, Johnson was a bit over-whelmed with Muir's nonstop conversation about his love of nature and the plight of the wilderness. Muir did not commit himself to a writing contract, but Johnson felt hopeful because Muir had invited him to visit the farm in Martinez.

When Johnson arrived in Martinez, Muir suggested that the two men tour Yosemite together. Johnson was enthusiastic about the idea and Muir was overjoyed. If this intellectual easterner could be convinced of the need to preserve Yosemite, then maybe all was not lost. The two men rode mules into Yosemite Valley, which awed Johnson. They then slowly wended their way through Tuolumne Meadows and up into the mountains as Muir waxed poetic about the natural features and stunning landscapes that surrounded them. They made camp at Soda Springs from where they took daily hikes to explore Yosemite on foot. Each day, the men explored a different part of the landscape. Although Muir made gentle fun of his much younger companion's lack of wilderness skills, the two got along famously. Johnson was stunned by Yosemite's breathtaking beauty.

At night, as they sat around the campfire, Muir talked about the damage that had been done to Yosemite by sheep grazing, logging, and other destructive human activities that were permitted by the state of California, which operated Yosemite as a state park. He spoke from his heart when he described how precious and irreplaceable the Yosemite wilderness was. One night after listening to Muir pour out his heart, Johnson made a simple suggestion. Why not work together to make Yosemite into a national park that would be protected forever? When he first heard this idea, Muir felt a spark of

OLD-GROWTH FOREST

After the destruction of the nation's eastern forests, the magnificent, ancient old-growth forests of the Pacific Northwest remained the country's greatest forest resource. The California Gold Rush had lured many enterprising Americans out West. Most of these prospectors failed to become rich, however, and many then found work in the growing timber industry. By the mid-1850s, the first four lumber mills had been built in Oregon. Twenty years later, 173 sawmills were in operation, turning clear-cut forests into lumber. Since then, almost all Oregon timber has been felled through clear-cutting, in which huge swathes of forest are denuded of trees.

Clear-cutting continued for decades. The loose soil that was washed down clear-cut mountains destroyed streams and fisheries. By the 1930s, there were 608 lumber mills and five paper mills in Oregon. With the invention of the chainsaw in 1935, clear-cutting moved into high gear, and Oregon became the country's number one producer of cut timber. By 1947, Oregon had 1,573 lumber mills that turned out more than 7 billion board feet of timber annually. Less than a decade later, most large-diameter, old-growth trees had been destroyed. Despite the Forest Practices Act, passed in 1971 to encourage sustainable forestry, clear-cutting continues in Oregon's forests. The National Forest Management Act, enacted hope. However, he then said he thought it could never happen and explained to Johnson the prevailing attitude of westerners about their right to use—and use up—the land for profit. No one in the West, he declared, cared about preserving natural beauty or wilderness.

Johnson thought otherwise. By the light of the flickering camp-fire, he told Muir that in other parts of the country attitudes about

five years later in 1976, discouraged but did not prohibit clear-cutting. Although some remnant old-growth forests are protected, clear-cutting continues, though yields are declining.

Clearcutting is a practice in which most or all of the trees in an area are cut down. Many environmentalists are against clearcut-ting because it destroys the natural habitats (food and shelter resources) of people and animals and it contributes to climate change. In this 1990 image, only a small grove of trees remains on top of a mountain in Willamette National Forest in Eugene, Oregon.

The tallest sugar pine tree is in Umpqua National Forest in Oregon. It is 265 feet tall (81 m) and 75 feet (23 m) in diameter.

the land were changing. Many Americans had been influenced by Thoreau and Emerson and, like Johnson (and Muir), were rejecting the "use it up and throw it out" attitude toward nature. In fact, many people were becoming alarmed at the degradation of so much of the nation's land. Johnson convinced Muir that the two of them were the perfect pair to save Yosemite. Muir would write essays about Yosemite and why it should be preserved while Johnson would lobby his influential friends and acquaintances in Washington, D.C. and New York to support the creation of a national park. Muir was skeptical, but he agreed.

SAVING YOSEMITE

As a prominent easterner, Johnson had very good connections, indeed. For example, he had friends on the public land committees in the U.S. Congress. As a magazine editor, he had great respect for the power of the written word. He was certain that Muir's impassioned writing would help sway Congress and the public to support an enlarged and protected national park in Yosemite. After all, there were precedents—for example, the creation of Yellowstone National Park in 1872. Johnson was certain that he and Muir would prevail over the timber and livestock interests that viewed Yosemite as public domain land that they could use in any way they wished.

Muir began writing his *Century* series of essays on the healing powers of nature. He wrote with eloquence and passion about the spiritual fulfillment people could find when immersed in wilderness. Then, as now, many people consider these essays about the awesome power of nature to be Muir's finest. For his first article, "Treasures of the Yosemite," published in August 1890, Muir wrote of his early wanderings in Yosemite and the Sierra: "From the heights [of] these glorious forests we at length gain our first general view of the valley—a view that breaks suddenly upon us in all its glory far and wide and deep; a new revelation in landscape . . . that goes far to make the weakest and meanest spectator rich and significant evermore."

In his next essay, "Features of the Proposed Yosemite National Park," published in September 1890, he focused on the most

sublime and beautiful areas in Yosemite. He also included a map of
the proposed boundaries of the park. In the collection *Nature Writings,* in the section of the essay on the Hetch Hetchy Valley, Muir
concludes that "Unless reserved or protected the whole region will

THE HISTORY OF PUBLIC DOMAIN
IN THE UNITED STATES

Public domain refers to lands owned by a government and, by
extension, the citizens of a nation. After the American Revolution
and the Louisiana Purchase of 1803, the new nation came to own a
vast expanse of land west of the Appalachian Mountains. The federal government assumed ownership of these public domain lands
in trust for the American people. Yet, the federal government did
not want to act as landlord to future settlers on these lands. So it
started selling or giving away public domain land to private property
owners. Laws, including the Homestead Act (1862), helped rid the
government of the land. By 1889, the great American frontier was
almost totally fenced in, and the frontier was officially pronounced
"closed." The issue of public domain was thought to be settled,
even though the government still controlled millions of acres.

People misused the land because the great giveaway was
based on the idea that the land existed solely for the purpose
of exploitation by citizens. This exploitation reached spectacular
levels, with enormous stretches of pristine wilderness sacrificed
to the greed of its "owners." Ruthless destruction of the land and
careless indifference to its condition or to the fate of anything living
on it became an American "value." Even for some today, the "right"
to use up and waste the land is seen as central to the definition
of what it means to be a "free" American. To this day, the federal

soon[er] or late[r] be devastated by lumbermen and sheepmen, and so of course be made unfit for use as a pleasure ground."

Meanwhile, Robert Johnson was back East, enlisting the aid of famous and powerful men, including Frederick Law Olmsted—the

government encourages this type of wasteful and destructive attitude. This attitude of greed and exploitation was especially strong in the West in Muir's day.

This September 2003 image of Chirikof Island in Alaska shows an example of overgrazed land. Ranchers often graze so many cattle on public domain land that all the grasses and shrubs are destroyed. Cattle also compact the soil, making it impossible for new plants to grow. Chirikof Island is now under the jurisdiction of the Alaskan Maritime National Wildlife Refuge, which has curbed cattle grazing.

man who designed Central Park in New York City. Olmsted was
an outspoken advocate for preserving areas of exceptional natural
beauty. He argued, rightly, that unless the government stepped in
to save these national treasures, they would be bought by wealthy
men and become private parks that were off-limits to the American
public. Americans, Olmsted insisted, deserved to have access to the
most sublime and beautiful landscapes in their nation.

Johnson and his powerful eastern supporters, including influential industrialists, continued to lobby Congress. Despite the odds
against it, in the autumn of 1890, Muir's map of the enlarged boundaries of Yosemite was included in a House of Representatives bill to
create the national park. Opponents of the bill tried to kill it, but
luckily the opposition was weak and disorganized. A similar bill
passed in the Senate. With little fanfare, in September 1890, President Benjamin Harrison signed the bill into law. Yosemite National
Park would be preserved for the nation and its people.

POWER IN NUMBERS

Despite his joy at the Yosemite victory, Muir's health continued to
deteriorate. Though his brother-in-law, John Reid, took over the
supervision of part of the family orchards in 1891, Muir still spent
much of his time laboring on the orchards. The pressure and tedium
of farm work was again taking its toll. With Louie's blessing, Muir
left for the Alaska wilderness, whose icy temperatures, he was sure,
would kill the germs that tormented his body. Once again, after
only a few days in the wild, Muir's cough was gone and he felt like
a young man again. His immersion in the Alaskan wilds brought
Muir sublime contentment, and he quoted Thoreau in his journal
that here "lies the hope of the world—the great fresh, unblighted,
unredeemed wilderness."

Unfortunately, soon after Muir returned to Martinez, his father-
in-law died. The Muirs now had to care for the elderly Mrs. Strentzel, who moved into the Muir household. Muir continued to manage
and improve the orchards. He was also engaged in a campaign to

enlarge the boundaries of Sequoia National Park, which had been created at the same time as Yosemite National Park. Muir felt overwhelmed by work and trapped by the responsibilities of life.

It had also become clear to Muir that his Yosemite essays had made him famous. Muir was surprised and a bit uneasy to find that his Yosemite victory had attracted a large number of admirers and supporters. He understood that the Yosemite success resulted from the activities of an organized group of people who were all dedicated to achieving the same goal. This success led Muir, Johnson, and San Francisco lawyer Warren Olney to mull over the idea of creating an organization that would promote preservation of the wilderness. Other like-minded people in the San Francisco Bay area were also interested in organizing some type of nature club that would work to keep commercial interests out of protected parks. They would also lobby for the creation of more parks.

The first meeting to formally organize this club was held in Olney's law offices in May 1892. The new organization was called the Sierra Club. On June 4, the club's founders unanimously elected John Muir as its first president. When Muir returned home from San Francisco, a close friend said that he had never seen Muir so happy. He had done something in his life that would last and that would help preserve wild nature for ages to come.

Life as a
Living Legend

With the Sierra Club up and active, Muir felt he could indulge his wanderlust. He decided to go on a journey to Europe that he had planned years before with his friend William Keith, but was unable to take. Finally, after Muir's brother David had taken over most of the work managing the orchard, Muir was free to go.

Muir arrived in New York City in the summer of 1893. Instead of immediately sailing to Europe, he was escorted by Robert Johnson to dinners and cocktail parties where—Muir was amazed to discover—he was treated as a celebrity. Everyone knew who he was and what he had accomplished. Everyone wanted to meet him. Among those he met were authors John Burroughs, Mark Twain, and Rudyard Kipling. Muir was a much sought-after guest because of his reputation and also for his charm and talent for storytelling. At each gathering, Muir spun spellbinding tales about his adventures in the Sierra and Alaska. His rapt audiences loved it.

In Europe, Muir visited Ireland, Switzerland, and England. The centerpiece of his trip was his return to Dunbar, Scotland. The

Writer John Burroughs (*right*) was among John Muir's famous friends. Burroughs was well-known for his powerful nature essays, often filled with wry humor and an awed view of natural resources. Here, they pose on Burroughs's seventy-fifth birthday.

town had changed little. Muir felt gratified that everyone he met had heard of him or had read his essays. Muir experienced a deep satisfaction as he revisited the places where he had wandered as a boy. He strolled along the harbor, visited the "haunted" castle, and roamed through the Lammermuirs.

CONFLICT OVER FORESTS

By 1896, Muir was hard at work on a book about his Alaska adventures. Yet later that year, he set this work aside to travel east to give the commencement address at Harvard University. Then Muir headed for Chicago, where he met with the other members of a forestry commission that the government had asked him to join. Forestry expert Charles S. Sargent had convinced President Grover Cleveland to form the commission to assess the state of the nation's western forests because of the widespread illegal logging and grazing that were destroying them. The commission would report to the president. Its members—Muir, Sargent, Gifford Pinchot, and three others—left for the Black Hills on July 5.

The commissioners assessed forests in Wyoming, Montana, Washington, Oregon, and Northern California. Everywhere they were confronted by the same devastation and waste. Huge expanses of forest had been burned for clearing. The High Plains grasslands they traveled through had been so overgrazed that they looked as though the soil might never recover. Wherever the forests and grasslands had been scorched or trampled and grazed, the topsoil had washed away, destroying the land's fertility while clogging up rivers and killing fish. The worst conditions were found on public domain lands, which westerners believed they had the right to use in a wasteful fashion.

A Falling Out

At first, Muir and Gifford Pinchot, his fellow commission member, got along well. They sometimes snuck away from the group to hike and explore on their own. They hiked the rim of the Grand Canyon and camped out under the stars. It seemed as though Muir and Pinchot would become friends. Yet as the deadline for preparing the commission's report drew near, it became clear to Muir that Pinchot's notion of what forests were for differed drastically from Muir's.

Muir was a preservationist, someone who believes that wilderness should remain unspoiled by humans and commercial exploitation. Pinchot, however, dismissed preservationist ideas. He famously explained his view like this: "The first principle of conservation is development . . . the use of natural resources now existing on this continent for the benefit of the people who live here now." Pinchot was a supporter of the practice of sustainable forestry. While he was not so crass as to promote the total annihilation of all the country's forests for short-term gain, he certainly did believe that the forests should be open to human enterprise and exploitation.

The commission members were split between Pinchot's group, which wanted the report to encourage resource use, and Muir and Sargent's group, which urged greater conservation and strict limits on human exploitation of forests. The

Gifford Pinchot served under presidents Theodore Roosevelt and William Taft as the director of the Forest Service. He later served as Pennsylvania's governor for two terms.

final report turned out to be a vague document whose compromises included allowing commercial use while setting aside forest preserves in which grazing would not be allowed. President Grover Cleveland accepted the report's recommendations and set aside 13 preserves encompassing more than 21 million acres (8.4 million ha) of forest. This act was the opening salvo in a land-use conflict that persists to this day.

WESTERN REVOLT

News of the establishment of forest reserves set off angry demonstrations in the West. In Deadwood, South Dakota, 30,000 people rampaged through the streets in protest because the Black Hills had been named as a preserve that they would not be allowed to exploit for its resources. Newspapers across the West denounced the reserves and called for state control of forests within their borders. The president decided to wait until things calmed down and postponed enactment of the law until 1898.

The revolt once again pitted the age-old American ideology of "wasting the wilderness" for profit and the need to conserve (or

GIFFORD PINCHOT

Gifford Pinchot (1865–1946) came from a well-heeled Connecticut family. After graduating from Yale University, where he studied forestry, he served in the fledgling U.S. Forest Service. He became the director of the Forest Service in 1898.

Pinchot knew everything about forests and trees—except how to value them for themselves. He believed in the efficient use of forest resources. Pinchot was not an outdoorsman. He viewed forests in terms of their economic yield, and he opposed illegal use of forests mainly because it was economically wasteful. As a young bureaucrat, Pinchot supported grazing on forest lands, a position that westerners applauded. In one of his speeches, Pinchot declared, "The object of our forest policy is not to preserve the forests because they are beautiful, wild, or the habitat of wild animals; it is to ensure a steady supply of timber for human prosperity." For Pinchot, the fate of forests was determined by a cost-benefit analysis of use and gain. Still, Pinchot recognized that to maintain that "steady supply" of timber, the nation's forests must be managed in a sustainable way.

In 1900, Pinchot helped establish Yale's famous School of Forestry. After leaving the Forest Service, he was twice elected governor of Pennsylvania (1923–27; 1931–35).

preserve) it. Most westerners rejected the idea that forests should be conserved for future generations or to retain the soil and prevent erosion and sedimentation of rivers. Nearly all westerners furiously opposed federal interference in their lives or federal laws that told them what they could or could not do with the land. It was a conflict over who could use public domain lands, how they would be used, and who would have the authority to decide.

Writing for the Defense

The vague commission report needed to be fleshed out by someone who knew about forests. The conservationists persuaded Muir to write articles in defense of forest preservation.

His first article, "Forest Reservations and National Parks," was published in *Harper's Weekly* in June 1897. In it, Muir explained how wasting the forest destroys the soil, the landscape, and the watershed. The second article, "American Forests," which appeared in the *Atlantic* in August 1897, appealed to the myth of America, or Americans' sense that their land had been specially blessed by God and so should not be destroyed.

In "American Forests," Muir wrote: "The American forests, however slighted by man, must surely have been a great delight to God; for they were the best he ever planted. The whole continent was a garden, and from the beginning it seemed favored above all other wild parks and gardens of the globe." Muir went on to say that the nation's forests "proclaim the gospel of beauty like apostles," adding that "they are rich beyond thought, immortal, immeasurable, . . . sheltering beast and bird, insect and son of Adam, . . . [having] . . . variety, harmony, and triumphant exuberance." Following these gorgeous descriptions, Muir tells of how they have been "scorched into melancholy ruins," but could still be saved. He concluded that "Any fool can destroy trees. They cannot run away . . . ," but only the American people can determine how to protect the forests. Muir's final article, "The Wild Parks and Forest Reservations of the West," published in the *Atlantic* (January 1898), described wild nature's healing powers, which were needed so urgently by toiling Americans who lived in cities isolated from nature.

In this 1902 image, John Muir rests in a forest. In an essay about the national parks, he noted that they were "places for rest, inspiration, and prayers."

THE PRESERVATIONIST AND THE PRESIDENT

Just months after being elected, President William McKinley was shot while on a trip to Buffalo, New York and later died. His vice president, Theodore "Teddy" Roosevelt, was sworn in as president.

Roosevelt was the nation's greatest proponent of wildlands conservation. He had great plans for conservation in the West, but before crafting conservation bills, Roosevelt sought out the opinions of experts in the field. John Muir was one expert he respected. Muir corresponded with the president, offering his views on how the government could help preserve America's forests and wild places.

Roosevelt named Gifford Pinchot head of the new U.S. Forest Service, and the president seemed to support Pinchot's views over Muir's. Roosevelt said in a speech that the "fundamental idea of forestry is in the perpetuation of the forests by use." Forests should not be carelessly destroyed, Roosevelt believed, but they should be used for the benefit of the nation.

In May 1903, Muir received a letter from Roosevelt asking if Muir would mind touring Yosemite with him. Muir agreed not because he was thrilled to meet the president but because he knew that the chief executive could help in the effort to preserve Yosemite. Muir prepared his own agenda of topics he wanted to discuss with Roosevelt, including the fate of western forests and the transfer of control of Yosemite Valley from the state to the federal government. Muir was particularly impressed with Roosevelt's request that the two men spend several days (almost) alone camping and hiking Yosemite.

Muir wore a new suit to meet the presidential train in San Francisco on May 14, 1903. The next day, the two men made camp in Yosemite's Mariposa Grove. From this base beneath the towering sequoias, the two nature lovers took extensive day hikes to see as much of Yosemite as possible. At night by the campfire, they talked about their love of the wilderness and of its fate. In Roosevelt, Muir found a man who loved the wild and had the outdoor skills to explore it. Each man thought the other a kindred spirit. They got along famously.

After four days in the wilderness together, Muir convinced Roosevelt of the need for federal control of Yosemite Valley. (Later, California would give control of the valley to the federal government and it would become part of the national park.) Roosevelt's view of forests also seemed to change. He had Congress extend protection to an area of sequoias and redwoods from Yosemite north to Mount Shasta. Roosevelt said that "it would be a shame to our civilization to let [these trees] disappear. They are monuments in themselves. . . . We are not building this country of ours for a day. It is to last through the ages." Muir was delighted and thought that Roosevelt now saw the land and nature as he did.

With this political goal accomplished, Muir set off on a round-the-world tour with his friend Charles Sargent. They visited Europe, which Muir found tiresome. In Russia, Muir became very ill but recovered sufficiently to travel to Siberia and Manchuria, both wild and unsettled places that revived his spirits. Then he headed for Shanghai, China, but quickly left to journey to India and the

THEODORE ROOSEVELT

Teddy Roosevelt (1858–1919) was born to a powerful and wealthy family. He was a weak and sickly child but as he grew older, he determined to overcome his weakness and to become a dedicated outdoorsman and hunter. After graduating from Harvard University, he served in the state legislature. However, he was shattered when both his wife and his mother died on the same day, and he withdrew from public life to live on a ranch in the Dakota Territory. It was here that his love of nature was confirmed, and he became a conservationist.

In 1886, Roosevelt returned to New York and served in many capacities in government. In 1898, during the Spanish-American War, he led the Rough Riders, a regiment that fought victoriously in Cuba. He came home a hero, which earned him the vice-presidential spot on William McKinley's Republican ticket.

Roosevelt became the nation's twenty-sixth president in 1901. He was a Progressive Republican who fought for "the little guy" and against big business, whose abuses he limited by government regulation. He became the country's greatest conservationist president. During his administration, national parks were expanded, national monuments were preserved, and wildlife refuges were created. Roosevelt fought for working people and for conservation throughout his two terms as president.

President Theodore Roosevelt (*fourth from the left*) poses with John Muir (*fourth from the right*) and others while on a tour of Yosemite in 1903.

Himalayas. The glorious, towering mountains capped by glaciers revived Muir's health and spirits. He rounded out the trip with tours of Egypt, Australia, and New Zealand. He returned home in May 1904, having been gone a year.

A TRYING TIME
Illness and Death

Muir's daughter Helen suffered from repeated bouts of pneumonia, for which her doctors recommended dry desert air as a possible cure. So, in 1905, Muir took both his daughters to live for a year on a ranch in the Arizona desert. Muir found as much to love and marvel at in the desert as he had in the mountain forests. Helen's health improved, but in June, Muir received a telegram from home stating that his wife had become gravely ill. Leaving his daughters in Arizona, Muir hurried back to Martinez where he learned that Louie was suffering from cancer. Muir remained by her side until her death on August 6, 1905.

Muir was devastated by the loss of his wife. His parents had already died, but no death brought him as much suffering as did Louie's. Though they had been apart for long periods of time, Louie knew Muir's soul, and he had loved her deeply. President Roosevelt sent Muir his condolences, suggesting that Muir spend time in the Sierra to heal his pain. However, Muir returned to Arizona to be with his daughters. He found particular comfort and peace in the stark and austere desert landscape.

In the spring of 1906, Muir and his daughter Wanda returned to Martinez. Their home seemed bleak and empty without Louie, but they worked together to build a new life. In June, Wanda got married, so Muir was now alone in the large and empty house. In August, Helen was sufficiently recovered to move back home to live with her father. She set herself the monumental task of organizing the thousands of pages of journals and notes her father had written over the past decades. Muir would eventually use this material in his books.

The Battle for Hetch Hetchy

In October 1907, Muir and his friend William Keith hiked to Yosemite, camping out in the Hetch Hetchy Valley. Muir explored almost every inch of the gorgeous, high-walled valley, which many thought more beautiful than Yosemite Valley itself. It is likely that at this time, Muir was preparing himself for the fight of his life, which he knew was near at hand.

Thirsty City

Since 1900, San Francisco had been scouting for a dependable source of drinking water. Hetch Hetchy was high on the city's list of sources. The Tuolumne River ran through Hetch Hetchy Valley, whose high rock walls and narrow outlet made it a perfect site for a dam and a reservoir for storing drinking water. The problem was that Hetch Hetchy was in a national park and so was considered untouchable.

In 1901, to remove this obstacle, a California congressman introduced a bill that would allow the Department of the Interior to grant permits to use national parks for dams, pipelines, and other water use structures as long as they were not "incompatible with the public interest." The Right of Way Act became law. Still, no action was taken to harness Yosemite's water until after the catastrophic earthquake that destroyed most of San Francisco in 1906. A great deal of the destruction in the city had been caused by fires, which made city residents more aware of the water problem than ever. Experts had testified that no water system could have survived the quake and prevented fire damage in the city. Yet now more than ever, the city demanded access to Hetch Hetchy.

Finally, Gifford Pinchot encouraged the city's mayor to reapply for a permit to dam Hetch Hetchy (previous permit applications had been turned down). In 1907, city officials resubmitted a petition to the Department of the Interior. In May 1908, the federal government granted the city the right to dam Hetch Hetchy. One reason given for this decision was that the Hetch Hetchy Valley was not really a unique feature of the national park, which was established primarily to protect Yosemite Valley itself.

Muir as Militant

John Muir immediately organized an offensive to stop the construction of the Hetch Hetchy dam. Muir felt that the federal action was a betrayal of the promise not to develop national parks. He feared that if construction of the Hetch Hetchy dam went forward, it would be a precedent for future destructive projects in national parks. He also felt the federal action as a personal injury. No one knew or loved Yosemite as he did, and it was through his efforts that the park was established in the first place. Muir had given up his life in the Yosemite wilderness to publicize the need to protect this land. Now, it seemed, he had given up the life he wanted to live only to have the land he loved drowned and destroyed.

As Muir wrote with increasing venom against the destroyers of wilderness, his reputation suffered. Many of those who had

John Muir poses circa 1909. At the time he was actively protesting the Hetch Hetchy Dam by writing articles, writing letters to presidents Roosevelt and Taft, and speaking with other politicians to protect the valley.

supported and believed in him now viewed his opposition to the Hetch Hetchy dam as selfish and narrow-minded. Muir was increasingly viewed as a crazed fanatic who was out of touch with "reality." Some of Muir's opponents characterized him as someone who would "sacrifice his own family for the preservation of beauty," or someone who loved trees more than people.

There are indications that Muir was obsessed by an unhealthy fanaticism during the years he fought to save Hetch Hetchy. He railed against the forces of development with the fury of an Old Testament prophet. He sometimes referred to the developers as Satanic, and is quoted as saying, "But what can you expect? . . . The Lord Himself couldn't keep the devil out of the first reservation [the Garden of Eden] that was ever made." In a 1906 interview, Muir was quoted as saying that people who did not appreciate the beauty of God's nature had "no right" to it and were not worthy of it.

Muir became so unyielding, even paranoid, in his views, that he even alienated many members of the Sierra Club, some of whom lived in San Francisco and supported the dam. Muir now saw these formerly devoted admirers as "enemies" who were allied with those who were betraying him and nature. Muir shunned the "traitors" in the Sierra Club by forming a splinter group he called the Society for the Preservation of National Parks, which organized a campaign to stop the Hetch Hetchy dam. Muir worked like a man possessed, which he was, but it soon became clear to the other members of the group that their case was hopeless. Muir felt totally alone and abandoned. In 1913, Congress passed the Raker Bill, which granted Hetch Hetchy to San Francisco, and President Woodrow Wilson signed it into law on December 19, 1913. The loss of Hetch Hetchy was almost unbearable for Muir. In a letter to his daughter Helen, he said that the pain of it was killing him.

Reconciliation

If he had allowed it to, the devastating loss of Hetch Hetchy would have emotionally destroyed Muir. His heart was filled with bitterness at the loss and the betrayal it represented. For a time,

Muir was overcome with anger and unable to forgive those who had "betrayed" him and the land. Muir suffered, as did his reputation. Americans questioned his love of the country and its people.

Before a dam was completed in 1923, the Hetch Hetchy Valley provided vast spaces of healthy grassland and towering peaks (*top image*). With the dam in place, the valley was flooded by the Tuolumne River, forming the Hetch Hetchy Reservoir (*bottom image*).

In what can only be described as a remarkable act of will arising from his strength of character, Muir forced himself to cleanse the bitterness from his soul. With a monumental effort, he turned his back on anger and turned toward life. He once again engaged with society and, in his old age, was recognized and adored as a national treasure. Reporters constantly sought interviews with him, following him everywhere he went. President William Howard Taft wrote to Muir requesting a presidential tour of Yosemite. In 1908, California named a magnificent grove of sequoias and redwoods Muir Woods in his honor. Muir's spirits improved, and he regained the love and respect of the American people.

In 1911–1912, Muir set forth once again to see the world. This time, he traveled through Africa and South America, regions he had wanted to see his whole life. In some ways, the journey—taken in the middle of the Hetch Hetchy battle—was a way to relax and escape from the bitter fight over Yosemite. In 1913, when he was back home, Muir was hard at work completing his autobiography, *The Story of My Boyhood and Youth.* Then he turned his energies to writing a book about his Alaska adventures, which he never finished but would be published after his death.

By 1914, the world was awash in the blood of World War I. As a result, there could be no foreign travel. Muir continued working on his Alaska book, but during the winter he became ill with the "grippe." Throughout his illness, Muir worked 12 hours a day on his writing. He occasionally took time off to visit his daughters, both of whom were married, and his grandchildren. That summer, Muir felt a sudden impulse to modernize his house in Martinez. He bought new furniture and had electricity installed.

In early December of that year, Muir visited his daughter Helen and her family who lived in Daggett, in the California desert. He traveled on a bitterly cold windy day. By the time he reached Helen's house, he was feeling ill. The morning sunrise seemed to revive him, but by evening, Muir was unwell again and collapsed trying to rise from a chair placed before the fireplace. A doctor was called, and he diagnosed Muir as having double pneumonia. Muir was placed on a stretcher and immediately taken by train to a hospital in Los Angeles, where he was admitted at 11:45 P.M. on December 23.

The next morning, Christmas Eve, Muir felt better. His health and his spirits improved as the day wore on, and he humorously chatted with the nurses and his family. As evening drew on, though, his condition worsened. During a moment when he was left alone in his hospital room, John Muir died quietly and peacefully.

Muir had long thought of death as a homecoming, and he had no fear of it. He had always understood death as part of the cycle of life, even a joyous part. He had seen how life springs from death, and so had no doubt that something of the living survived after death. "The grand show is eternal," he once said. "It is always sunrise some-where; the dew is never dried all at once; a shower is forever falling; vapor is ever rising. Eternal sunrise, eternal sunset, eternal dawn and gloaming, on sea and continent and island, each in its turn, as the round earth rolls."

Muir's Legacy

Without doubt, some type of environmental movement would have emerged in the United States even if John Muir had never lived, or if he had spent his whole life in Scotland. Nevertheless, the focus of American conservation would probably have been very different because John Muir was the spirit behind the movement to *preserve* wild natural landscapes. He inspired and invited Americans and other people from around the world to experience the wilderness and become one with it. Without Muir, the United States would likely have only commercially developed conservation areas.

Muir was not the first to praise the value of immersion in wilderness to the human spirit. Years before him, Henry David Thoreau wrote about this in his books *Walden* (1854) and *The Maine Woods* (1864). Nor was the Sierra Club the first conservation organization. In 1886, the great conservationist George B. Grinnell founded the Audubon Society to support bird conservation. The Audubon Society bought and protected land that was habitat for threatened birds.

ECOLOGY AND WILDERNESS

In the decades following Muir's death, the science of ecology gained respect. Some ecologists pushed for the protection of entire ecosystems, the complete array of plants, animals, and nonliving things that exist together in large areas. Maintaining healthy populations of plant and animal species required preserving whole, undisturbed ecosystems. Thus, science supported Muir's preservationist view of nature.

Unfortunately, most ecologists at that time spent their days in the lab dissecting dead animals and plants in order to classify them. Most of them seemed unconcerned about the vanishing habitats that the animals and plants they were studying needed in order to survive. One ecologist, Victor Shelford, opposed this narrow view of ecology. He firmly believed that it was ecologists' duty to save unspoiled ecosystems—or wilderness. Shelford organized the Committee for the Preservation of Natural Conditions, which later became The Nature Conservancy. The Conservancy identifies and buys ecosystem land that is vital to the survival of threatened plants and animals. By protecting entire ecosystems, the Conservancy, in its way, follows in the footsteps of John Muir.

A "New Deal" for the Land

During the Great Depression, President Franklin D. Roosevelt created the Civilian Conservation Corps (CCC) to put millions of unemployed people to work "improving" public lands. Beneficial work included planting trees in logged-out forests. Road-building, however, was one of the harmful initiatives organized by the CCC. Thousands of workers were paid to cut dirt roads through national forests and other unspoiled areas. These roads made it much easier for logging companies and other commercial interests to gain access to these former wilderness areas. To Roosevelt, the main objective was jobs. He did not consider the impact that these projects would have on wild lands.

Robert Marshall, an official at the U.S. Department of the Interior, was an enthusiastic supporter of Roosevelt and the New Deal. But his first love was unspoiled nature. In many ways, Marshall was the first inheritor of John Muir's spirit and his love of the wild. Marshall worked at the Department of the Interior where he promoted his ideas about preserving the wilderness. In one speech,

ROBERT MARSHALL

Bob Marshall grew up in New York City, the son of a rich lawyer. Summers he spent in the country ignited Marshall's lifelong love of nature. At age 12, he climbed his first mountain. He was also a "marathon" hiker, routinely covering 30 miles (48 km) per day. His love of the woods led Marshall to study forestry in college. After graduating, he spent a year wandering the wilds of Alaska. Like Muir, he wrote about his adventures there.

Marshall first chose a career in the Department of the Interior, as chief of forestry in the Bureau of Indian Affairs. In that job, he tried to undo the unholy alliance between the agency and the lumber companies. Marshall opposed Gifford Pinchot's forest policy. He felt that some forests should be kept off-limits to destructive human activity.

Marshall later became Director of Recreation and Lands in the Forest Service. In this capacity, he set regulations limiting road construction and development on more than 14 million acres (5.6 million ha) of national forest land. In 1937, he created 16 wilderness areas, and he stopped commercial development along the 2,000-mile-long (3,219 km) Appalachian Trail.

As a founder of the Wilderness Society, Marshall fought to protect lands that were "the environment of solitude" and "a human need rather than a luxury or plaything." Here again there are echoes of Muir. Though Marshall died young, he was honored when a Montana wilderness was named after him, a place affectionately called "the Bob."

Marshall named Muir among his list of "greatest" Americans. He once wrote that "A person might die spiritually if he could not sometimes forsake all contact with his . . . fellow men, and the machines which they had created, and retire to an environment where there was no remote trace of humanity." Muir could have written these lines.

While he was on official business in Tennessee in January 1935, Marshall met with fellow preservationists to create The Wilderness Society, a group like no other. The Wilderness Society promoted the preservation of untouched wilderness, forever free of development or exploitation. Muir would have been proud.

Aldo Leopold was one of the most prominent members of the Wilderness Society and another inheritor of the Muir spirit. Born in Iowa in 1887, Leopold had loved to hunt, and he had made a career of game management. But his love of hunting soon disappeared. Leopold realized that wildlife eradication programs—aimed at killing off wolves, bears, mountain lions, and coyotes—were harming other animals and their ecosystems. In his *Sand County Almanac,* Leopold wrote with wit and passion about humanity's responsibility to conserve the land and preserve wilderness and its creatures. With Thoreau and Muir, Leopold is among America's greatest nature writers and one of its strongest voices for preservation.

Like Muir, Leopold defended the intrinsic worth of every living creature. His conversion from hunter to preservationist arose in large part from the universal hatred and killing of wild predators that was—and to a great extent still is—rampant in the land. Then, as now, the federal government funded a program for killing predators that might harm livestock raised by sheep- and cattlemen. Predator-control programs extended their reach into national parks and other supposedly "protected" natural areas. Timber and mining companies used their political clout to get the government to open wilderness areas to resource exploitation. Millions of acres of public wilderness lands were destroyed for private profit. These conflicts continue today.

American conservationist and ecologist Aldo Leopold, shown here in 1947, was the first professor of wildlife management at the University of Wisconsin.

MUIR'S CHILDREN

The conflict between conservationists/preservationists and resource exploiters is as fierce today as it was in Muir's day. Yet new leaders have emerged and adopted Muir's vision. Though for years it had been weak and ineffective, by the 1960s, Muir's Sierra Club had become a national powerhouse of conservation action under the leadership of David Brower. Brower was a great leader with a strong personality and a total dedication to Muir's ideal of wilderness preservation. In the 1970s, Brower, a passionate advocate for wilderness, left the Sierra Club to form Friends of the Earth, a group that was even more insistent in its campaign for wilderness preservation.

By the 1970s, when the first Earth Day was celebrated, increasing numbers of Americans supported conservationist ideals as they began to feel uneasy with the "consumer society" they lived in. They realized that owning more "stuff" did not make them happier. They saw that sprawling suburbs were eating up farmland,

THE ARCTIC NATIONAL WILDLIFE REFUGE

For years, oil companies have been drilling for oil off the northern coast of Alaska at Prudhoe Bay. Preliminary testing has shown that there is also some oil—though probably not very much—east of Prudhoe Bay in a nature preserve called the Arctic National Wildlife Refuge (ANWR). ANWR is a vital nesting ground for many species of birds and a crucial calving area for a large herd of caribou. It is also one of the last truly unspoiled natural wildernesses in North America.

Nearly every year, someone in Congress proposes opening up ANWR to oil exploration and drilling. Each time this proposal is made, many Americans write letters to Congress insisting that ANWR be protected from the oil companies.

The ANWR case is important because it shows a change in many Americans' attitudes toward wilderness—an attitude Muir would approve of. ANWR is so remote and so wild, Americans know that they have almost no chance of ever going there and experiencing it. Yet, even though it is out of reach, they still want it preserved in its pristine state. After two centuries of wilderness open space, parks, and even wild places. They worried that soon there would be no nature left. For these and other reasons, the majority of Americans advocated saving nature and wilderness for its own sake.

Deep Ecology

While many Americans embraced Muir's ideas of wilderness protection, there were some who went further. The Deep Ecology movement not only advocates for wilderness, it teaches that humans must live in harmony with nature. Deep Ecology, though considered

exploitation, most Americans have had enough. With too little wilderness left, Americans want to make sure that what remains is preserved as wild nature forever. The American public has begun to value wilderness as Muir had done.

The Arctic National Wildlife Refuge in Alaska is the largest national wildlife refuge in the United States.

by some to be a fringe group, is in fact most closely in tune with the ideals of John Muir.

The term *deep ecology* was coined by philosopher and professor Arne Naess in a 1973 article in the journal *Inquiry*. Naess wrote that a new religious and philosophical worldview was needed if humanity was to solve its environmental problems and live in harmony with the earth and all creatures on it. The basics of deep ecology could have been lifted directly from Muir. They include creating an ecological consciousness in oneself that is open to the solitude, silence, and richness of unspoiled nature and determining to live as part of nature.

Deep ecologists embrace one of Muir's central beliefs: that the Earth was not made for humans to use up. According to writer George Sessions, "Ecology teaches us that mankind is not the center of life on the planet. Ecology has taught us that the whole earth is part of our 'body' and that we must learn to respect it as we respect ourselves. As we feel for ourselves, we must feel for all forms of life." On April 21, 1984, the anniversary of John Muir's birth, Arne Naess published a list of the basic principles of deep ecology: living in harmony with nature; honoring the intrinsic value of all life; viewing oneself as part of and equal to, not above, nature and other living things; living simply and reducing one's material needs because Earth's resources are limited; recycling and reusing materials; using nondestructive technologies; and protecting biologically rich regions. In sum, deep ecology asks people to concentrate on the quality of their life within nature, not on the quantity of things they accumulate.

For deep ecologists, as for Muir, love of nature can be a type of religion in which one rejoices in God's creation and, by honoring and preserving it, praises God and His work on Earth. There can be little doubt that if he were alive today, John Muir would be a deep ecologist. He lived his life as the first deep ecologist, and the movement honors him above all other lovers of nature. Sessions acknowledges deep ecology's debt to Muir: "Muir inspired the deep ecology movement by asking significant questions of his own life and of the human species. Can humans limit themselves and reverse the path of destruction done in the name of progress, exploitive economic development, and warfare on Nature itself? The word *ecocide* had not been coined during Muir's lifetime, but he certainly understood the concept and its implications."

The words of Henry David Thoreau also convey the essence of John Muir. "I went to the woods because I wished to live deliberately, to front only the essential facts of life, and see if I could not learn what it had to teach, and not, when I came to die, discover

John Muir called his home office the "scribble den." This desk is where many of his important essays were written. Today, the home where Muir spent the final 24 years of his life is part of the John Muir National Historic Site in Martinez, California.

that I had not lived. I did not wish to live what was not life, living is so dear; nor did I wish to practice resignation. . . . I wanted to live deep and suck out all the marrow of life, to live so sturdily . . . as to put to rout all that was not life, . . . if it were sublime, to know it by experience."

Perhaps no one experienced the deliberate life at one with nature more deeply, more profoundly than John Muir. Writing in his journal during his early days in Yosemite, Muir exclaimed, "Our flesh-and-blood tabernacle seems transparent as glass to the beauty about us, as if truly an inseparable part of it . . . a part of all nature, neither old nor young, sick nor well, but immortal."

How to Get Involved

Joining any of the following organizations will help you get involved in saving wilderness and wildlife.

American Forests

734 15th Street, NE, Suite 800

Washington, D.C., 20005

Phone: 202-737-1944

Web site: www.americanforests.org

American Forests is an organization that is mainly concerned with promoting policies that preserve the forests of the United States. American Forests supports laws that prohibit exploitation of forests and that set aside and preserve wilderness forests.

Conservation International

2011 Crystal Drive, Suite 500

Arlington, VA 22202

Phone: 703-341-2400

Web site: www.conservation.org

Conservation International is a large organization that protects and preserves wilderness and wildlife in the United States and around the world. It is involved in creating wilderness preserves in many countries, especially in areas where endangered species live. The group employs scientists who research the ecology of endangered species and who work with governments to set aside national parks and other types of wilderness preserves. The organization is also involved in many issues that affect wilderness and wildlife. Information is available on their Web site.

The Nature Conservancy
4245 North Fairfax Drive, Suite 100
Arlington, VA 22203-1606
Phone: 703-841-5300
Web site: www.nature.org
The Nature Conservancy raises money to buy unspoiled land in the United States. In addition to protecting wilderness lands, it also restores wild lands that have been degraded to bring them back, as much as possible, to their natural state. The Nature Conservancy owns and protects numerous preserves throughout the United States, many of which the public can visit.

Save the Redwoods League
114 Sansome Street, Suite 1200
San Francisco, CA 94104-3823
Phone: 415-362-2352
Web site: www.savetheredwoods.org
The Save the Redwoods League works to preserve the West's remaining redwoods by raising money to buy areas of forest under threat of development or exploitation. It also has a program that helps restore disturbed redwood and sequoia forests through plantings, brush removal, and other activities. The group engages in research and also advocates for policies that preserve redwoods and other forests.

Sierra Club
85 Second Street, 2nd Floor
San Francisco, CA 91405
Phone: 415-977-5500
Web site: www.sierraclub.org
The Sierra Club was founded by John Muir, and it continues to uphold his values and his legacy. The Sierra Club fights for the preservation of wilderness, for non-exploitation of public lands and wild lands, and for saving wildlife and endangered species, among other environmental issues. It also organizes a wide variety of wilderness

hikes and trips. You can sign up for its newsletter on the Web site to stay informed about its activities and issues.

The Trust for Public Land
101 Montgomery Street, Suite 900
San Francisco, CA 94104
Phone: 415-495-4014
Web site: www.tpl.org
The Trust for Public Land purchases wild lands and open space that it preserves and manages. The group saves both wilderness lands as well as open space and parks in and around urban areas.

The Wilderness Society
1615 M Street, NW
Washington, D.C. 20036
Phone: 202-833-2300
Web site: http://wilderness.org
The Wilderness Society acts to protect and expand areas of wilderness in the United States. It advocates for the preservation of existing wilderness areas and for the creation of new ones. It monitors use of wilderness to prevent commercial exploitation. The group is also involved in the protection of species that need the wilderness to survive.

Chronology

1838   John Muir is born on April 21 in Dunbar, Scotland.

1849   Daniel Muir and his sons, John and David, immigrate to Wisconsin in the United States; establish Fountain Lake farm.

1857   Daniel Muir buys new farmland; the family moves to Hickory Hill farm.

1860   John Muir exhibits his inventions at the State Fair in Madison, Wisconsin; meets Jeanne Carr for the first time. Abraham Lincoln is elected president; the South secedes from the Union.

1861   John Muir matriculates at the University of Wisconsin, Madison. The Civil War begins.

1862   Muir is introduced to botany by a fellow student. He becomes an avid botanist and plant collector.

1863   Muir leaves the University of Wisconsin.

1864–66 Muir travels to Canada, where he wanders and botanizes in the forests and wetlands around the Great Lakes. During the winters, until 1866, Muir works at a sawmill.

1865   Muir and Jeanne Carr begin a regular correspondence.

1866   Muir finds employment at a wood-working factory in Indianapolis, Indiana, where his ingenuity is recognized and he is made foreman. He invents new, more efficient machinery.

1867   Muir is temporarily blinded when he accidentally pierces his eye with a sharp file. While recovering, Muir decides that his destiny lies in the wilderness he loves, not in manufacturing or invention.

Muir begins his 1,000-mile (1,609 km) walk to Florida and the Gulf of Mexico, intending to travel from there to South America. Muir contracts malaria, which forces him to cancel his plans for South American travel.

1868   Muir travels to California. He immediately leaves San Francisco for the mountain wilderness of the Sierra. Muir sees Yosemite for the first time.

The Carr family settles in California.

1868–69   Muir works as a shepherd for "Smoky" Jack. He continues to study botany and geology in the Sierra.

1869   Muir spends the whole summer in the Sierra, working for Pat Delaney as an overseer of shepherds. He spends most of his time exploring and botanizing.

1869–73   Muir lives almost continually in Yosemite, exploring and becoming one with nature.

1871   Muir publishes "Yosemite Glaciers" in the *New York Tribune.*

Muir is convinced by Jeanne Carr to publish his study of glaciation in Yosemite.

Muir tours Yosemite with Ralph Waldo Emerson.

1872   Muir begins writing for the *Overland Monthly.*

Yellowstone National Park established.

1872–73   Muir's writings are in great demand, and he continues to publish articles about Yosemite.

1874   Muir's continuous residence in Yosemite ends.

1874–76   Muir conducts an intensive study of the trees of Yosemite.

1875   Muir lives with the Swett family in San Francisco, and also explores the southern Sierra.

1876   Muir publishes "God's First Temples" In the Sacramento *Record-Union.*

1877	Muir explores the Great Basin with eminent scientist. Late in the year, he returns to San Francisco and lives with the Swett family. He continues to write and lecture on his nature and science.
1878	Muir moves to Martinez, California.
1879	Muir becomes engaged to Louie Wanda Strentzel.
	Muir undertakes his first trip to Alaska.
1880	Muir marries Louie on April 14.
	Muir makes his second expedition to Alaska, making important observations of glaciers.
1881	Muir takes over the orchard and learns the fruit business; he becomes quite successful.
	Muir travels to Alaska for a third time.
	Muir's daughter, Annie Wanda, is born, March 25.
1882–87	Muir manages the Martinez fruit farm, which becomes highly profitable.
1884	Muir makes his only trip to Yosemite in the company of his wife.
1885	Muir's father, Daniel, dies.
1886	Muir's second daughter Helen is born, January 23.
1888	Muir climbs Mt. Rainier.
1889	Muir helps in the creation of Yosemite National Park, mainly through his writings.
1890	In October, Yosemite is officially named a national park.
	Muir writes two articles for Johnson's *Century* magazine.
1891–92	Muir is relieved of managing the family fruit farm.
	Muir organizes the Sierra Club and becomes its first president.
1893	Muir visits the Chicago World's Fair and travels to Europe, including Dunbar, Scotland.

1894	Muir publishes his first book, *Mountains of California.*
1896	Muir's mother dies.
	Muir travels with the Forestry Commission.
	Muir again travels to Alaska.
1897	Muir travels to Alaska once more.
1899	Muir's last trip to Alaska.
1901	Muir writes to President Teddy Roosevelt about the importance of preserving land in the West.
	Muir writes *Our National Parks.*
1902	Muir, with the Sierra Club, begins fight to save Hetch Hetchy.
1903	Muir camps with President Roosevelt on a tour of Yosemite.
	Muir begins a world tour to study trees.
	Jeanne Carr dies (December 14).
1905	Louie Muir dies (August 6).
	Yosemite comes under the control of the federal government.
1906	Muir explores Arizona and the Petrified Forest.
	Muir continues his fight to save Hetch Hetchy Valley from damming.
1908	Federal government grants Hetch Hetchy Valley to San Francisco.
1909	Muir publishes *Stickeen.*
1911	Muir publishes *My First Summer in the Sierra.*
1911–12	Muir travels to South America and Africa.
1912	Muir publishes *The Yosemite.*
1913	Muir publishes *The Story of My Boyhood and Youth.*
	Fight to save Hetch Hetchy is lost; the valley is dammed.

1914	World War I begins.
	John Muir dies on December 24 in a Los Angeles hospital.
1915	*Letters to a Friend* and *Travels in Alaska* are published.
1916	*A Thousand-Mile Walk to the Gulf* is published.
1917	*The Cruise of the Corwin* is published.
1919	*Steep Trails* is published.

Glossary

alpine   Referring to mountains, as alpine meadows

botany   The scientific study of plants

clear-cut   A form of logging in which all the trees in a given area are cut down

commodity   Something intended to be traded or bought and sold for money

conservation   The principle or act of saving something from being destroyed

deforestation   The destruction of a forest, usually by cutting all its trees

ecocide   The total destruction of an ecosystem (related to words such as genocide, meaning the destruction of a specific people)

ecology   The scientific study of how plants, animals, and nonliving things function and interact in their environment

ecosystem   The interactions among all the living and nonliving things in a specific place; a system that functions because of the interaction of all its component parts, including living things and nonliving things, such as rocks, soil, weather, etc.

erosion   The wearing away and removal of topsoil, such as by the wind or water

extinction   The total disappearance of a species from the Earth; when all members of the species are gone

fertile   Referring to soil that has lots of nutrients and other beneficial things that help the growth of healthy plants

flywheel   A heavy wheel used in machinery whose turning rate controls the speed at which the machine works

geology   The scientific study of the materials and processes that make up the Earth, such as rocks, the interior of the Earth, etc.

glaciation   The process in which a glacier covers part of the land

glacier   A large mass of ice that moves slowly over the land

habitat   A place that contains all the things necessary to support the life of particular plants or animals

hostel   A rough, simple, inexpensive type of lodging

naturalist   Someone who studies plants, animals, and other aspects of nature

old-growth forest   An ancient forest whose trees have been growing for hundreds of years or more

parasite   An organism that lives off and harms another organism

preservationist   Someone who seeks to preserve wilderness in a form untouched by people or any type of development

provisions   Supplies, such as food

revival   In Christianity, a movement in which people gather to pray, sing, and receive the spirit

sawmill   A place where a saw cuts felled trees or logs into lumber

schooner   A fast-sailing ship with two sails

sect   In religion, a group that breaks away from the main religious body to worship and believe in a new and different way

sedimentation   The process where soil that has washed off the land is deposited in lakes, rivers, and other bodies of water

species   A group of organisms that can interbreed to produce fertile offspring

sustainable   Refers to a way of using resources so that they are not used up and destroyed but are maintained for future generations

sylvan   Referring to a forest or woods

terminal moraine   The forward edge of a glacier where it deposits all the rocks, soil, and other things it has picked up during its forward movement; when the glacier melts, these objects are left at the terminal moraine

terrain   Landscape; the shape of the land, such as flat, mountainous, etc.

watershed   All the land that drains into a major water body, such as a river

weathering   The process in which wind, rain, and ice wear down rocks, eventually turning them into soil

Bibliography

Fox, Stephen. *John Muir and His Legacy: The American Conservation Movement.* Boston: Little, Brown & Co., 1981.

Gisel, Bonnie Johanna (ed). *Kindred and Related Spirits: The Letters of John Muir and Jeanne Carr.* Salt Lake City: University of Utah Press, 2001.

Heacox, Kim. *Visions of Wild America.* Washington, D.C.: National Geographic Society, 1998.

Turner, Frederick. *John Muir: Rediscovering America.* Cambridge, Mass: Perseus Publishing, 1985.

Wilkins, Thurman. *John Muir: Apostle of Nature.* Norman, OK: University of Oklahoma Press, 1995.

Further Resources

BOOKS

Adams, Ansel and William A. Turnage. *Sierra Nevada: The John Muir Trail.* Boston: Little Brown & Co., 2006.

Cornell, Joseph. *John Muir: My Life with Nature.* Nevada City, Calif.: Dawn Publications, 2000.

Ehrlich, Gretel. *John Muir: Nature's Visionary.* Washington, D.C.: National Geographic, 2000.

Muir, John. *Stickeen.* Whitefish, Mont.: Kessinger Publishing, 2004.

Stetson, Lee (ed). *The Wild Muir: Twenty-two Tales of John Muir's Greatest Adventures.* Berkeley, Calif.: Heyday Books, 2008.

WEB SITES

John Muir Association

www.johnmuirassociation.org

The John Muir Association exists to celebrate the life, work, and accomplishments of the great advocate for wilderness. The site contains information about Muir, a photo gallery, and news about their activities intended to promote wilderness preservation.

John Muir Historic Site Museum Collection

www.nps.gov/museum/exhibits/jomu/index.html

This Web site also covers the John Muir Museum Collections Exhibit, which contains more background information on Muir, as well as photographs and writings.

John Muir National Historic Site

www.nps.gov/jomu

This Web site contains information about the preserved Muir home in Martinez, California. It also provides information about Muir's life and work, including some excellent photographs.

John Muir Writings

www.yosemite.ca.us/john_muir_writings/

This Web site contains nearly all of John Muir's writings, including his books, articles, essays, and other miscellaneous jottings. The Web site is a treasure of insight into John Muir's work and spirit.

Sierra Club John Muir Exhibit

www.sierraclub.org/JOHN_MUIR_EXHIBIT/

This part of the Sierra Club Web site contains a biography of Muir, as well as many photographs of him and the wild places he visited. The site also provides some of Muir's original writings, and the writings of other naturalists who describe Muir's contributions to wilderness conservation in the United States.

Picture Credits

Index

About the Author

NATALIE GOLDSTEIN is a long-time writer of nonfiction books for children and young adults and has been a science writer for more than 20 years. She has master's degrees in education from the City College of New York and in environmental science from the SUNY College of Environmental Science and Forestry. She has written several science books on topics ranging from global warming to vaccines, as well as books on globalization and religion and the state. She has also written extensively in science, health, language arts, and history for textbooks prepared for elementary school, middle school, and high school audiences.